Signposts to Source

My Path to True Love and Alignment

By Laura Morrice

Dedication

This book is dedicated to everyone who is or has ever felt lost from their path or their purpose. You hold all the answers, you just have to journey within, to follow your signs.

Laura Morrice, Energy Alignment Healer and Coach,
www.lauramorrice.com

Contents

Acknowledgements

To Mam and Dad, without you, I simply wouldn't be who I am today. Thank you for your love and support, for giving me the space to make my mistakes and learn from them, and then to help pick up the pieces when I needed. I love you.

To Glen, my husband, my rock, my soul mate, I'm graterful we found each other again, and that I get to do life with you, and yes, it was your idea that I should write this book. Thank you.

To my brothers, there may be physical distance between us but our bonds are strong, I love you both.

To Theresa, my Murray Minter, my partner in crime, thank you for always being there and for helping to set this journey in motion. And to Xavier — I always knew I was leaving her in good hands…shear it!

To Norma, my friend and Reiki master, thank you for committing me to my path of love and light and for your continuous support and guidance.

To Suzana, I can't imagine our paths not crossing. You held me accountable, so I'd stop playing it small! You are one of the truly pure souls in this world; keep shining your beautiful light.

And to everyone who I ever gave my power away to, thank you, because without you, I would have never discovered my true worth, my internal power, or my life's purpose.

FOREWORD
~
By Suzana Mihajlovic

It is my honour to write this forward for Laura Morrice's debut book, *Signposts to Source*. I have known Laura now for several years, and I cannot speak highly enough about her, first and foremost as a person, but also as one of the most talented healers that I have ever met.

Laura is such an attractive and loving force. Being in her presence, even if it is only virtually, instantly leads to a feeling of calm, love, and a connection to a naturally higher frequency that is difficult to express in words. I have often shared with Laura that she reminds me of a living Angel, and that about sums Laura up.

I travel the world frequently in my role as a mindset specialist and elite level success coach. No matter where I am, Laura has this incredible ability to reach me with her energy. It is something extraordinary that I have not experienced before. There have been numerous times when Laura's been able to do an energy healing session with me whilst I am in Toronto, Vancouver, Los Angeles, Melbourne, or Queensland Australia — all the way from her home in Scotland. She always seems to be able to connect with the block in my energy centers, and each time, I have been left with a feeling of release and energy flowing freely through me.

I have been to many healers, and I can confidently say that Laura is the best I have personally experienced. Her ability to connect from and with her heart is superb. Her ability to understand and to heal is a gift that I believe is an innate part of who she is.

I was thrilled when Laura shared with me that she had completed her book because it is clear Laura's purpose is to reach people all over the world with her talent. She has a major part to play in this life and in the healing of our marvelous planet. This candid book is one way that Laura will continue to help heal many with her gift. Laura practices what she preaches, and in this book she openly and generously shares her life story and connects with the reader on a deep level. Her sometimes difficult life experiences, and the way she has shared them in this beautifully written book, reveals a new awareness that we are all on this life journey to heal. We are all here to fulfil a deep and very important purpose, and by connecting with the Universe and the signposts that present themselves in our daily experiences, sometimes the most grueling daily experiences, we can all open up and experience our own connection to Source and fulfil our magnificent purpose.

Thank you, Laura, for this beautiful gem you have gifted the world. Your heart will continue to travel near and far in many places, healing our wondrous planet one person at a time. Your sharing of experience naturally allows all of us to open up and be more of who we are.

Introduction

For so long, I lived a life that was out of alignment, feeling that something was missing, searching for the answers — for wholeness. I had this internal knowing that there was more to life, and the more I pushed to find what it was, the further away from myself I got. This pattern of pushing against my inner gut feelings would repeat itself over and over again. Like a hamster running endlessly on a wheel, trying so hard, covering so much distance (or so I thought), only to find that I was running in the same circles. They just had different disguises.

It took a long time for this reality to really sink in. My life took so many detours, and I experienced so much pain and hurt before the veil lifted and I was finally able to see the bigger picture. One day, I finally had the lightbulb moment that forced me into taking action to break the cycle and regain control. My moment of insight came when I was tired of feeling lost, hurt, and helpless. I was tired of fighting back the tears that were constantly threatening to spill.

My light bulb moment came 11 years ago now, and since then, I've been working persistently on my energy alignment, my mindset, and my perception. I can now see how the choices I've made have shaped me into the person I've become; I can also see how and where social conditioning has affected me. Of course, this is true of everyone. But one of the biggest things that enabled me to turn my life around completely was that I took responsibility for ALL of my actions. It was then that the pieces of my life's puzzle began to make sense. I was able to see how they formed part of a bigger picture, one that I hadn't been able to grasp while swimming around in a pool of desperation and drowning in self-pity and despair. In one moment of pure clarity, I heard, and more importantly, felt a truth that had been in my sub-conscious since long before I was born into this reality. That realisation was that EVERYTHING IS ENERGY, resonating at different frequencies, and the basic fabric of all energy is...LOVE.

One of my mottos has always been, "Never say never," yet I never envisaged myself writing a book. But because I have learned over time to *feel* my way through life, I've been able to read the signposts that Source has presented to me. Over the last year or so, the calling for me to put pen to paper became so deafening that I couldn't ignore it any longer.

We all have a story to tell, and this book is a collection of some of my life experiences and how they've led me back to the natural state of alignment — more clarity, less confusion; more flow, less hardship — so I can enjoy a life with its foundations built on love, joy, and happiness. I want to share these stories with you because I know that everyone is meant to live a life based on the qualities of love and positivity, not fear and struggle. It is one of my greatest desires that one day we all vibrate from a place of pure unconditional love, not in a hippy-hug-a-tree kind of way — though I am quite partial to hugging a tree — but because it is right for us, and it is part of our purpose. We all deserve to enjoy the diversity that the world has to offer. Our desires are as unique and individual as we are, and as long as they are pure and cause no harm to others, why should they remain out of our grasp? That would defy the purpose of creation, and we have all come forth into a reality that has creation at its very core.

My journey as a healer began over twenty years ago, and as I look back, I can see that I was always being gently guided toward working with people, to help bring them an understanding of their physical and non-physical energy bodies, and to align with wellbeing. I was meant to help them navigate their path back to love and wholeness through self-discovery. A combination of Reiki, crystal healing, and mindset work has been the backbone of not only my own personal development but also that of most of my wonderful clients. None of the tools that I work with will act as a magic wand. The solutions that I offer here will yield you results, but the outcome will be based entirely on the amount of love, time, and work you are willing to invest in yourself. I can promise you this: whatever you want in this life can become a reality for you. In fact, they can become far greater than you ever imagined. All you have to do is commit yourself, put in the time and effort that is required to crush and demolish the old paradigms that do not serve you, and replace them with new, positive behaviours and a mindset that will ultimately change your life for the better — for your highest and greatest good.

My life could have been so different. I became an addict and got involved with toxic people and relationships that only fuelled a downward spiral of victimisation and self-doubt. Trust me when I say I was riding the rapids of despair, and I could have easily fallen overboard and drowned in them. But in that moment of realisation that I had, I remember thinking, *"If all I get out of this is a little more positivity, then I've already won!"* And that was all I needed at the time to turn everything around — and I do mean EVERYTHING.

In the last eight years, I've re-connected with and married my soul-mate, healed old wounds, and released so much fear-based thinking — some of which I'd been carrying around with me for more than half my life. I've manifested our perfect family home and a career I'm passionate about, but above all, I've found the alignment my soul has been searching for, which has gifted me faith — faith in Source, in myself, and faith in the knowledge that we are all connected by a higher energy.

The contrasting situations that we all have to face in life are still there, but now my life's course is not dictated by a negative reaction to what happens. I am in control of how I react by what I think, as we all are. Through changing my mindset, I have learned how to stop myself from reacting when life throws me a curveball and thoughtfully respond instead. We always have a choice; the difference lies in whether we choose a positive or negative reaction based on how things make us feel. Since I decided to match my vibrational energy to the things that create positive emotions in my life, I gained the inner confidence and courage that allows me to go from strength to strength. I no longer compare myself to others or doubt my ability. There's no more struggle or repetition of patterns that yielded mediocre or even no results. Now I experience ease and flow. I feel love and appreciation for everything that comes my way. I no longer see things as obstacles but as opportunities for growth, and I feel truly blessed.

Energy never dies; it continues to grow, change, and evolve, and this physical reality that we experience through life (that we all signed up for) doesn't stay still. You see, in terms of energy, nothing is ever created or destroyed, it just is, and it isn't limited by the confines of space and time — everything exists simutaneously. But in our physical reality that we experience as day to day life, there are limits. We see and feel time as a very real thing through day and night time passes, we age and eventually pass on from this existence. The past is gone, the future isn't promised to us, so the present moment is all that there truly ever is. With that in mind, can you afford to keep living a life that, through a misaligned conception, holds you in the shadows of fear? Do you have the time and energy to waste going around in the same circles, pushing hard yet getting nowhere? Can you afford to feel anything other than complete wholeness and satisfaction in the life that you lead?

It is one of my firm beliefs that when the majority of people find their alignment and start living, not merely existing, the collective consciousness can make its next evolutionary leap, and that gets me excited! That's what gets me out of bed in the morning determined to be better than I was the day before. It's what inspires me to see how and where I can serve others, to walk my talk, and help others to do the same.

I invite you to read my story, to offer love, inspiration, and encouragement for finding the energy alignment that is right for you. To help open your inner and outer vision so that you can recognise and read your signposts to Source, so that you can experience the sensation of a return to wholeness right now. Because your time is now!

CHAPTER 1

~

Finding Me Again

I spent roughly six years in a relationship that I knew wasn't right for me — six years! I never expected it to go on that long, and looking back, I know that I was ignoring the signals my mind and body were giving me. I was refusing to follow my inner guidance. Ultimately, this relationship cost me not only a huge amount of time but also myself. I lost myself completely. My self-confidence, self-respect, and personal power were stripped away until there was nothing left, and this wasn't the first time this had happened in my life.

It hadn't always been like that, but if I'm completely honest, it's a relationship that I wasn't ever really aligned to in a romantic sense. We had been good friends for about a year, and there was a strong bond between us. I loved him, but I was never in love with him. So why did I allow the relationship to develop into something I knew it wasn't? One word — fear. My relationship choices hadn't worked out well for me before, and here was someone that I knew thought the world of me, so after thinking about the reasons why I suppressed that inner voice, I concluded that it was because I thought I couldn't or wouldn't get hurt by someone who was already such a close friend. In hindsight, I realise why this logic is flawed; although friendship is really important when it comes to romantic relationships, on its own it simply isn't enough, not for me anyway. I need to connect with someone on every level — emotionally, mentally, and physically — and I didn't. I thought I could do without the physical connection and attraction and that our strong friendship was enough. I am also aware that even though I was in that relationship, I hadn't properly healed from a previous one that had also been based on fear, albeit in a completely different context. But, more on that later.

I remember sitting one night, feeling the loneliest I had ever felt in my life. We had been together for around four and a half to five years, but the truth of the matter was we should have gone our separate ways after a few weeks or months because we weren't compatible in a romantic, intimate sense, as far as I was concerned, but I did have a lot of love for him in a platonic way. I think we didn't want to hurt each other's feelings by admitting that our relationship was a mistake. So time passed, and we found ways of coping and blocking out the truth, so that we didn't have to face it. The music that he listened to over and over was beginning to grate on me, his lack of action and excuses to back up his lethargy in all areas of life now made me resentful and angry. By this point, we were continuing to go through the motions of our relationship, but neither of us was happy, and neither of us wanted to do what deep down we knew needed to be done. There I was in my living room with my partner, not a word being spoken between us, and as he sat there drinking beer and listening to music with headphones on which had become the norm for weeks (I mean, come on Laura, the signs were so clear), I began to wonder what on earth I was doing with my life, and what had become of me.

As I sat there, a voice inside me asked, "What is it that makes you tick, Laura? What gets you excited about life?" As I searched for an answer, I realised that I didn't have one. I couldn't think of a single thing that really got my juices flowing when there had once been so many.

My heart started to race, and I felt a wave of sadness come over me as the truth of my situation hit me like a ton of bricks. I didn't know who I was anymore. Through not following my gut instincts for so long, I had lost myself and become a shell of the person I used to be. Even *I* struggled to believe that I was once a person full of positivity, effervescence, and a zest for life. I felt like a failure — pathetic and weak — and this was hard for me to accept.

Over the next few days, I began to work through the emotional scale with the reality that I was facing. I felt depressed about most things in my life — my partner, my surroundings, all that I lacked — and I started to get angry with what was going on around me. This led me to look for people and things to blame. Inwardly, I blamed my partner; it was his fault my life had become so shit! He was the one that was dragging me down with him. He was undriven and always full of excuses. He never

3

took responsibility for his actions. This train of thought helped me start to figure some things out, but really, playing the victim was getting me nowhere; all it did was keep me going round in circles in my head, having one-sided conversations that, ultimately, served no purpose. This turning point in my thinking was the beginning of the end of my relationship, but it still took about six months from this point for the break to manifest.

One night, I went to visit my best friend, Theresa. For weeks she'd been raving about a DVD that we just had to watch, and this was the night that the Universe decided I was ready to realign with a forgotten truth. We got comfortable on the sofa, she pressed play, and on came *The Secret*. There had always been a knowing inside of me that we all came here with a purpose and that we are all connected to everything, but I had never dived into this idea fully before. I suppose I was always too busy looking outside myself for guidance. Within a few minutes of watching, I had a major 'AHA!' moment. Everything just fell into place and made sense. The mess that was my life was ALL my own doing, I had created it all, and I had just kept on adding fuel to the train of negative momentum that I was riding. The moment that I took responsibility for my actions was the moment I had been waiting for. The clarity that I now felt, the personal power that had been missing from me for so long, came back with a BANG. It suddenly hit me:

EVERYTHING IS ENERGY. EVERYTHING IS CONNECTED. I CREATE MY REALITY!

I understood then that my feelings and emotions had always been there to guide me, but because I ignored them, my life snow-balled out of control, and I got caught in a vicious cycle. But not anymore. My inner fire was now lit. I felt a connection to my Source energy that I hadn't felt for a long time. I was in control of my life — well, to be more precise, my thoughts and emotions were — and this made me feel excited and whole again.

This change in perception would be the beginning of my journey of self-discovery. I was ready to dive deep into me, deeper than I'd ever gone before. Some of the emotional healing I'd already experienced was just scratching the surface of what I'd have to uncover to understand the bigger picture of my life and how it had brought me to where I was. I craved this understanding, and I knew then that nothing would stop me in the search for it. You see, as much as I love the non-physical, spiritual awareness of life, I need to balance it with a sense of logic, so it makes sense and I can learn and grow from the experiences I've had. One thing that I've come to understand clearly is that we are forever learning, forever growing and evolving. Nothing is set in stone, and that includes our perception. Awareness of your present moment is one of the most valuable skills you can develop, and it's only activated through a desire to live a life of alignment to our inner truth.

Faced with what I needed to do, I made a promise to myself that I would do the work that came up for me to find that feeling of alignment I was seeking, never again to feel anything except an appreciation for all that this wonderful life has to offer. Like most things in life, it's never as straightforward as we imagine it to be. The new chapter I was beginning would require me to go back over some of my past, but the insights gained from this process would be priceless and would turn on my internal compass, so that I would never ignore it again.

My main goal now was to make a conscious decision to care about my thoughts, and more importantly, to care about my feelings. I was still in my crap relationship, but I knew this wouldn't last, and I knew that I didn't have to do anything; it would take care of itself because my point of attraction had shifted. The more I put myself first and kept the positive momentum going, the more the negative people, situations, and things stopped appearing in my life. My partner started to see the difference in me; he started to see that strong woman I once was re-emerge, and he didn't like it. I think it reflected the same fears I had come up against in him, and I could tell he was starting to feel threatened by it.

I started meditating again after watching *The Secret*. I had done some meditation while at college but never made it part of my routine. The first night I did it, I was blown away, and I knew this was going to be the start of something amazing for me. I sat on the edge of my bed, feet planted firmly on the floor, closed my eyes, and began by taking three very deep breaths. I could feel tingling sensations all over my body. I started to feel the most relaxed I'd ever felt. My breathing returned to its natural rhythm. I was aware that my body was following this with a gentle swaying action, and it amplified the connection I was feeling to the non-physical part of my being. Next, I put my focus and my intention on my heart chakra, to open it up to give and receive unconditional love to all life. I imagined a flower bulb, right in the centre of my heart chakra. Now it was important for me not to push for a visual. I had to hold the intention and whatever came would be right for me at that time. And what appeared in my mind's eye, couldn't have been more perfect; it was a wild, giant daisy. The vision of this flower was so clear and so detailed, I could sense the feeling of its soft and slightly velvety petals. I could smell the gentle, sweet fragrance, as though I was holding one under my nose. The daisy was dancing in a gentle breeze. The vision I got that night was so poignant to me. The beauty of this wildflower represented my true state of being. I was stripping myself back to the knowledge that I was, at heart, a wildflower, capable of bending in the winds of life without breaking, free from any internal or external restraints. I had diluted my passion for life and with that my strength, but this was a turning point in my alignment with my higher-self. I spent about twenty minutes in this meditative state, and what a wonderful first experience it was.

When I came out of the meditation, I remember the sensation of heat travelling up my body, from my feet to my head. It was so overwhelming that I had to lie down as a rush of nausea accompanied my euphoria. I heard a voice saying, "It's alright, Laura, just let your body catch up." To say I was buzzing from this experience was an understatement, so naturally, I wanted to share it with my partner.

His reaction was initially very deflating. I could sense his fear that it was only a matter of time before I returned to being the strong-headed woman I was when we first met. I knew that bitterness and resentment weren't far behind because when you start to level up, not everyone will be happy for you. Change forces others to face up to things they don't always want to confront, and if they aren't ready to make a change within themselves, they'll try just about anything to sabotage your efforts, or make you feel guilty for wanting it for yourself.

The months passed and things were breaking down between us more each day. Whenever I was around him, I would burst into tears because the tension was getting so bad. Comments like, "I can't take you being like this no more," to which I replied, "I can't take living like this no more." We started to speak about going our separate ways. By this point, neither of us could ignore the fact any longer. The air was growing increasingly stale around us, yet I was determined not to push for the solution. I knew the Universe would provide the perfect one, and it did. He announced that he was moving out — going to try something else, somewhere else — and this suited me just fine.

I did not feel ready to leave the home, partly because I felt my time there was not finished, and partly because I loved it, so I stayed. It was on a farm just a mile or so from the local town. There was a stream by the side of the house, which was crucial for my inner healing. So many times, I sat by that stream meditating, putting my broken pieces back together. I also loved my neighbours. My ex and I had many mutual friends, having been together for such a long time, and I didn't want to be bumping into him, so his decision to move away was music to my ears. The day he was moving out, even before he'd left the house, I started to redecorate and reorganise. I didn't do it to be nasty, it's just that I had been waiting so long for this change, I had to implement it immediately; I had to create harmonised energies around me, this much I knew, and I was determined to listen to my inner knowing, having ignored it for so long. I was learning to put myself first again. My feelings and well-being mattered again, and it felt good.

As soon as he was gone, my momentum started to flow once again in a positive direction. I saw the shift in my mindset was working for the better already. With my dad's help, I set up my own business doing mobile beauty and complementary therapies. I'd been in beauty since I was eighteen, and I knew I was an excellent therapist. It took less than four weeks for me to get everything organised, and within six weeks, I had already attracted enough clients to keep my head above water. This was a huge deal for me. I was slowly but surely reclaiming my power and allowing more faith in the fact that I was an extension of Source energy, that the Universe not only wanted me to succeed but was guiding me along the perfect path to do just that. Every day I meditated and devoted time to affirmations and visualisations, and these are tools that I have used every day since.

The time I spent travelling to and from clients was great for affirmations. At times, I could get myself so involved with them, I'd be screaming them at the top of my lungs! People driving past me must have thought I was crazy, but I didn't care. I was shifting my old thought patterns and replacing them with new ones that served me. Every day, my actions were rewarding me with positivity in every aspect of my life. I was happy from the inside out, and this happiness wasn't attached to anything or anyone. I felt this way because I'd decided that nothing was more important than how I felt. I thank Abraham Hicks for that saying every day, and I encourage you to keep it in mind too; whenever you feel that disconnection from your true state of being, say it to yourself over and over: *"Nothing is more important than how I feel!"*

So I had a new focus in life: me and my wellbeing. I was enjoying life again, enjoying this journey of inner discovery, and loving how my business was going from strength to strength and attracting a lot of new clients, all of whom were genuinely lovely people. I had a great list of regular clients, and then I also started to attract high-end clients who owned private estates scattered across the Highlands. I loved these high paying gigs — and not just for the money. The people were fascinating, kind, and encouraging, plus I got to travel pretty much all over the Highlands of Scotland. Now for those of you who have never seen the Highlands of Scotland, it truly is one of the most stunning parts of the world you will ever see. The raw, rugged beauty is spectacular, the jaggedy mountains and deep swooping valleys with rivers cutting through them, leading to lochs, surrounded by heather hillsides that turn the most vibrant shade of purple towards the end of summer — not to mention the wildlife that left me in awe. There were many times when I was driving along a single track road only to turn the corner and be greeted by wild deer, standing or lying on the road. On one particular trip to Durness, there were so many stags on the road I had to stop the car and wait for them to move on. To sit there amidst such wild beauty, and to have these magnificent creatures trust me enough to get so close to me, was a true honour. It was clear that they were calling the shots and would move when they were good and ready, but I felt no fear. Our respect was unspoken and mutual. We connected, and I feel forever humbled and blessed for that day and for that experience.

Occurrences like this became usual for me; sightings of certain birds or animals started to serve as indicators as to how well my vibration matched with my Source energy, sometimes even insights into what was about to manifest in my life. The Highlands and its wild inhabitants, especially birds of prey and deer, played a huge part in my healing, in helping me to gain clarity and alignment. And they continue to this day, with the addition of a few new species. Life was good, I felt happy, and my happiness soon turned to excitement, though the reason for that was unclear at the time. Something was brewing, and I couldn't wait to find out what the Universe had in store for me.

CHAPTER 2

Enter, Reiki

A good friend of mine had been to get her first attunement to Reiki, and I already knew that this was something I would probably end up doing. I'd always loved the concept of it, and it fitted in with my philosophy that everything is energy. This was a way to get to know that non-physical energy better, not only for myself but for others too. I had done so much personal development work of my own, and I had reached the point where I could do no more without some guidance and a push in a new direction. It had been about four years since I'd had my first taster session of Reiki, and the time felt right for me to go and get some more, so I booked in for a single session with a Reiki Master. I didn't have any real expectations, other than it would help realign my energies, but at the same time, I could sense that this was part of the excitement that had been building within me. There was something more to this.

It was around the beginning of 2009 that I went for my first Reiki attunement. I had been studying and living according to the principles of the Law of Attraction for approximately eighteen months. Things were going well in my life. I felt good, and I had a purpose. I had been free of my toxic relationship for almost a year, and I could feel that something new was waiting on the horizon.

Norma lived not far from me — approximately a half hour drive, depending on the weather. The journey up to her home was a particular favourite of mine. Alongside the Dornoch Firth, the road twisted and turned through breathtaking scenery. It didn't matter if the weather was nice or not because the colours, the contrast, and everything you would see on the drive was inspiringly beautiful. Once you got through the small village, about ten miles from where she lived, the roads became even more winding, and a cluster of rivers gathered in what is known as the Kyle of Sutherland. The roads are single track, so there is only room for one vehicle at a time and you have to pull into passing places to let other drivers by. One could easily be forgiven for believing that the fairytale like Glens are full of fairies and magic. The old wisdom of the Celts and Pictish whispers in the breeze. I enjoyed the drive up to Norma's as much as her company, and to this day, when I drive along that ethereal road, which sadly isn't very often now, it still has that same healing effect on my soul. It's the old familiarity that feels so soothing. Even as I type these words, I can conjure up the sensation of how it feels to be in the heart of that magical land.

My first drive up was at dusk, just as the sun was going down. The scenery was dark and moody. I'd finished up a bit earlier with my clients that day, so I could schedule in some 'me' time. As I turned the last corner, before arriving at the property, there was an area of tree clearances with a couple of remaining ones standing. My gaze was averted straight to the tallest tree on which sat a huge, beautiful, regal buzzard. I slowed the car right down to savour the sight of her, and as I did, she gracefully flew down and swooped right over the bonnet of my car before flying along the road in the direction I was going. I drove the 600 yards or so to the opening and there, perched on the gate post, was the buzzard. It was such a poignant and beautiful sign from Source — I mean, there was no mistaking that I was meant to be there for this Reiki session — that my higher self, and my guides were all waiting for me. I was right where I was meant to be, and I knew it. My excitement and anticipation were now going full steam ahead, and tears of joy rolled down my cheeks as I pulled up into this sanctuary for my soul.

As soon as I laid eyes on Norma, it felt like I was greeting an old friend. I could tell our paths had crossed before in previous lives. I felt at ease immediately, so I told her about the buzzard outside, to which she smiled knowingly and said, "They've been waiting for you all day." Thinking back now, I should have been more overwhelmed by this statement, perhaps even somewhat questioning, but instead I was calm and accepting because I knew innately that it was true. We went through the consultation formalities, and then I got onto the treatment bed where Norma proceeded to lay out a crystal grid beneath me and then on my chakras.

I quickly felt my body sink into the treatment bed, and within minutes, I became so relaxed and heavy that I could not feel any part of my body, except for my head. I focused on the intention — to be open to the energy — and nothing more. I held no expectation, truly surrendering to the moment before I floated away. Normally, I find it hard to switch off during a treatment as I'm just too aware of what is going on around me, but not this time. All I remember is a deep feeling of bliss as I admired a kaleidoscope of bright, vivid colours in my mind's eye, shades of purple and green and the brightest white I could imagine, with specks of golden flakes through it. There were a couple of times that I felt like I was floating and as though my body was trying to rise off the bed, and I enjoyed those sensations. I felt the vibrations of my non-physical energy like I was meeting up with a part of me I had forgotten. Exactly what was going on around me, I am not sure, for I was travelling through time and space reuniting with more of my inner truth that had been waiting for me to show up. I don't know how long my session lasted for exactly, but I know it was longer than Norma or myself had anticipated. When she brought me back into the room and I opened my eyes, I saw that she was sweating profusely. "Wow," she said.

She asked how I felt, and grinning like a cheshire cat, I told her I felt amazing. I sat up feeling groggy and heavy, both physically and mentally — but in a good way. I felt completely restored, and I knew that after going to sleep that night, I would awake in the morning feeling re-born. I told Norma about the bright colours and the sensation of floating away, to which she responded by saying, "Yes! Yes you were." She told me that she'd had to literally pull me back and ground my energies to the here and now, that my connection and awareness of Universal energy was very strong, but that I had to focus on grounding my energies in the physical reality, in order to make the most of my connection and raise my consciousness and awareness even higher. She said I would have no problem at all with astral projection and connecting with my guides, but first, I had to work on my lower three chakras and balance them with my upper four. From what I experienced during my treatment, all of what Norma said to me made perfect sense, and I knew from that moment, I would be back to learn Reiki and become a Reiki Master myself. I knew that this was part of my journey, something I was being called to do. I said this to Norma, and she agreed. She said that some people were born for it, and she could feel that I was destined to become attuned to Reiki energy. Before I left, she gifted me two crystals; one was a piece of falcons eye and the other a piece of selenite. She told me, "These two want to be with you and will bring the balance between your lower and upper chakras when meditated with." This was the icing on the cake for me; the falcon's eye really does look like a bird's eye, and as I stared into it, I could feel I was being watched over. It was a sign of protection and assurance that I could trust my instincts and that I was on the right path.

Before I left that night, I scheduled another appointment for two weeks and said that we could discuss the Reiki course in detail then. Two weeks felt like a long time to wait — I wanted to get started then and there — but I knew I had more work to do on myself, first. I left with an excited heart because I had opened myself up to a stream of Universal energies, and I knew that it was just the beginning. How the journey would unfold from there on, I did not know, but I revelled in the wonder of it and knew it would be life-changing. I could feel that I was aligning with my purpose. I felt a happiness inside that I'd never known before, and that was empowering.

Over the next two weeks, I committed to working on my lower chakras. Every day, I spent extra time meditating, centring and grounding my energies, before turning my focus onto the two crystals I got after my Reiki session. I felt the acceleration in my spiritual development straight away. I was ready to devote time to me, to go inwards for the answers I was seeking. It was the start of two years of self-discovery on my part. I had no idea how far down the rabbit's hole I would have to go, or how much of my past I would have to re-visit, for the growth that I wanted and needed to take me forward in my path of discovery. To move ahead in life with anything, we need to be anchored firmly into the physical reality, for we are all spiritual beings in a physical vessel. Our body is the vessel in which we get to ride out this magical journey. Getting to know your vibrational frequency intimately is a must for finding your unique alignment, and one of the easiest ways to do this is to do your own centring and grounding exercise daily. You can include it at the start of any meditation, or it may be done as a meditation on its own. It's especially nice to do in bed at night before you fall asleep. Any time I've astral projected (when your consciousness leaves your body, and you're capable of travelling through space and time), it has been while doing this exercise, but never have I managed to astral project with the deliberate intention of doing so; it just doesn't work like that, so my advice is to try and not force these things. If they are meant to happen, they will. Enjoy your meditation time but never expect or intend anything other than to create space in your mind for calmness and clarity. I know many people who have been meditating for years, and they've never experienced astral projection. At the end of this book, in the Resources section, I've included a gentle and beneficial centring and grounding exercise that I enjoy doing. It is a simple, meditative technique and is suitable for even those new to meditation. I highly recommend giving it a go and making it a regular part of your daily self-care routine. I've also included a Chakras Guide for those of you who might be wondering what on earth I mean when I mention them.

CHAPTER 3

~

Black Elk

The 20th May 2009 was the day I received my Attunement in the First Degree of Reiki. All my training was done on a one to one basis over three days; I wanted it like this rather than in a group setting. This was part of my spiritual development, and although I knew this was a tool for helping others as much as myself, I needed to be selfish with the time I had with my Reiki Master. I needed to be able to focus on my learning alone, and this would also ensure that the pace of learning suited me, with no distraction from anyone else.

I was full of excitement as I navigated those familiar, winding, beautiful roads to my first day of training. As I drove, doubts started to creep in and disrupt my flow of positive energy. *Can I do this? What if I'm not able to feel or sense the energy? Am I going in the right direction with this?* My ego was doing its best to sabotage my thoughts, to convince me to stay in my safe zone and reject the natural evolution that life had been navigating me towards. I'm laughing at the thought of my doubt now because, just as I turned that last corner, there she was again, perched high on top of the last tree standing in the clearance: my buzzard.

Within a second, the doubt disintegrated, and I knew that this, just like the last time, was a sign from Source. It was the Universe's way of saying "YES, Laura, you are on the right path, and you CAN do this!" I slowed the car down again to get a good look at the buzzard, and just like before, she swooped down and flew right over the bonnet of my car. I cried tears of joy. There's nothing like the feeling of true knowing within you, to have so much certainty and clarity, to feel the connection to your Source. And that's what the signs do — they confirm things at a deep cellular level within us. You don't have to justify or share them with anyone; they are your signposts, guiding you in the direction that is best for you at that moment in time.

In the beginning, we need these signs and the feelings of security they provide us. Eventually though, you become more acutely aligned with your internal compass that you stop looking for — or needing — the physical signs. You learn to listen to and trust your intuition. The signs will still present themselves, like when the Universe is trying to give you a heads up about something, but your reliance on them will decrease.

After my training and attunement, I began my twenty-one-day Reiki cleanse. As the name indicates, this involved performing Reiki on myself every day for twenty one days, for a minimum of 30 minutes. I loved this process and did it first thing every morning and last thing every night. I found it very empowering, and every day as I did it, I felt like I was becoming more authentically ME. It was as if my soul had been waiting for my physical body to catch up to it. The colours and sensations that I would feel as I was channelling this Source energy amplified constantly. I was developing deeper connections with my non-physical being, and that, in turn, would strengthen the connection between my physical and non-physical self, increasing my intuition, and creating crystal clarity in my thoughts. From this clarity came an ever-increasing urge to piece together the past experiences and situations that had led me to where I was at that point in time. It had begun well over a year before, during my light bulb moment, as I watched *The Secret*. The very second that I stopped playing the victim in my life and started accepting responsibility for my actions and choices was a turning point in my understanding of why things had been the way they had.

So, life was going well — great in fact! My business was going from strength to strength, and my appointment diary was always full. For the first time in what felt like forever, I could pay all my bills and have money left over! I could buy myself new clothes, pretty items for the house, and anything else I wanted. For the first time in so long, I wasn't merely surviving. I was living. If I wanted to book a holiday, I could do so — guilt-free. Since starting to apply the law of attraction, I had deliberately stopped myself from having a *lack mindset* in any area, and although I'd always managed to keep my head above water since going it alone, this was the first time that my cup was being filled up, and it felt good. I could see and feel the results of the personal development work I had been doing, people around me could see the difference, and I felt like an unstoppable force of nature.

Within seven weeks of my First Attunement, I was back receiving my Second Degree in Reiki. I hadn't planned for it to be as quick as that; my Reiki Master had said that normally she would allow at least six months between a First and Second Attunement, but her guides had instructed her to offer me the chance to do it earlier, so it was an offer that I wasn't going to refuse, and this felt like another sign from the Universe that I was heading in the right direction with its full support. Because I was taking any action that I could for my life to evolve the way I wanted it to, the Universe was helping my manifestations to come to fruition faster than I had anticipated. Because I was ready, vibrationally aligned with who I had become, the flow was smooth and at a pace I could easily manage, so at no point did I feel overwhelmed by all the action taking. The timing was perfect. I wasn't trying to push, and I wasn't trying to control anything; I was living in the moment. Yes, I still had dreams and desires and things I wanted to create, but this relationship that had developed between my physical and non-physical being was the sweet spot for understanding how and when to act. It was the return of me being able to trust my intuition.

During my First-Degree training, Norma guided me through a meditation during which I met with my Reiki Guide, and it was such an amazing experience. I was in a misty forest, and as the mist cleared, there in front of me was a man. He was quite tall, had a stalky kind of build with white hair, and a full white beard. He was wearing long, blue, simply designed robes and a small brown leather satchel. He didn't speak, just looked at me then gestured for me to follow him. We took off through the trees, following a winding path. I remember I had almost to run to keep up with him. He was very quick and light on his feet, given his rather heavy build. We got to a river that was flowing at a gentle but steady pace, and at the side where we stood was a beautiful, natural pool formation, with large boulders around it. Despite the silence, I could sense the man's gentleness. He directed me to sit down on one of the boulders, and when I did, he took off my shoes and began to wash my feet in the pool of water. I sat there in amazement at what was happening; I didn't truly understand it but was reminded of Mary Magdalene washing Jesus' feet. It was a very humbling experience. As this gentle stranger washed my feet so lovingly, a part of me felt unworthy of such a gesture, but at the same time, I felt honoured. After washing my feet, he wrapped them in muslin and left them to dry, put my shoes back on, and instructed me to stand. Then, we set off back in the direction that we'd come from, through the trees, along the winding path, all at great speed again, until we reached the spot where he had first appeared to me. He gently took my hands and nodded, and then he turned and walked off into the trees again. As he did, I asked him, "What is your name?" He replied quite simply, "Yolande," and continued on his way, disappearing into the trees.

As I came round from the meditation, I didn't know what to make of it, but I knew that something profound had just happened. I told Norma what I had experienced, and she was very happy and excited for me. We spoke about how it seemed like it was a cleansing ritual for me, preparing me for a life of spiritual awakening by accepting Reiki into every aspect of my life. It would be a few weeks before Yolande would return and make sense of my experience with him, and when he did, well, it would blow my mind more than I could have ever anticipated.

Seven weeks passed between my first and second Reiki training, and in that time, I was completely consumed with it. I couldn't get enough of the energy, the learning, the growing and evolving. I was still self-treating every morning and practising on friends any chance I got. I was also delving deeply into learning about my chakras and meridians. Although I'd covered these topics before through studying reflexology, I wanted a truly profound understanding of the bridge that they formed in connecting our physical and non-physical bodies. The more I worked with them in my being, the greater my self-understanding was in every area. For the first time in my life, I could feel the subtle fibres in life's energies that connected everything; I was so appreciative that Reiki had come into my life. This was no 'flash in the pan' experience for me but a lifelong commitment to embracing the Universal energies that we are all a part of and that make up everything.

During my Second Degree training, we were covering the Reiki symbols, and I had to do a meditation in which I laid down on the floor on top of a huge power symbol. This was another meditation in which I would go to meet my Reiki guide. I was excited. I hadn't met with Yolande since our first encounter. I was hoping that he'd be there, but I tried not to put any expectations on the experience and just focused on being aligned with Source Energy. As the mist cleared again, there he was, standing at the edge of a forest, and just like the last time, he was silent. Still, he gestured hurriedly for me to follow him through the trees, and so we went again, quickly following that winding path that led me into a tent in the middle of the trees. As I turned to look for him, he was gone. He seemed to have vanished without a trace, so I sat in the tent, and before I could look around me, a large figure rose from out of the ground and appeared before me. Dressed mostly in black, and with a full feathered Indian headdress on, its deep voice announced, "I am Black Elk, and I am a powerful medicine man. I am here to be your Reiki guide. Your power lies in your hands and your heart, and I will show you how to use your power." He then touched the centre of my head — my third eye — with his first and middle finger, and as he did, my entire body fell back, and I was out of the meditation.

I wept with joy. I had heard of Black Elk, knew he was a real person that had walked this earth, and it was this fact that blew me away. As I shared my experience with Norma, she again just smiled knowingly. During my first Attunement she had seen a single bald eagle feather go in through my Reiki channel, so she was unsurprised by what had just happened. I now realised that Yolande wasn't my actual guide, rather he was guiding me to my guide, Black Elk, who had been waiting patiently to see how committed I was before making himself known to me. The whole experience that I'd had with Yolande became clearer. The foot washing ritual was cleansing me and preparing me for my path, but it was a path I had to walk along for myself. First, I had to take the daily steps to increase my connection and allow more Universal energy into my daily life. It had to become a part of who I was. I can always sense Black Elk's energy around me during Reiki sessions, and sometimes my clients even see him or hear him, but when he wants to communicate with me, it is always on his terms. Without warning, I'll be taken off somewhere during meditation, and he will appear, giving me pieces of information or guidance on how to perform something new in my healing sessions. I like the surprise element of our relationship, and what he gives me is always timely.

I've paid homage to him by having a bald eagle feather tattooed on my left wrist. I wanted to acknowledge the connection of his spirit with mine. It's a daily reminder of the connection that we all share — that we are all one. It's also a reminder that we are all part of a much bigger picture, and when we tune in to the natural forces that surround us, we can see and feel the guidance that is always there for us. When we become true to ourselves, there is nothing that can stand in our way, nothing that can cause us to feel fear, and nothing that can make us forget that we are beings of love and light.

CHAPTER 4

❧

Crystal Clear

It would be roughly a year until my final training and attunement for becoming a Reiki Master. But before that, I would embark on a journey into the kingdom of crystals — a journey that would force me to re-visit my past. It would be a trip back to truly understand the direction of my life's path, to understand the meaning of unconditional love, and to confront the fears that I thought I'd released at their root. Had I known what was in store, maybe I wouldn't have been so eager to charge ahead, but that's the beauty of the Universe and its energies, it always knows the easiest path for us to take in order to get our heart's TRUE desires. And it will never place something on our path that we are not capable of dealing with.

For as long as I can remember, I've had a fascination with crystals, but it wasn't until I began my Reiki practise that I got seriously involved with them. I had purchased my first crystals in the form of a simple chakra necklace about 20 years earlier. I was discovering the chakra system at the time, so I knew very little about it, but somehow that necklace spoke to me, and I wore it every day until the thread eventually snapped. It was the start of my spiritual development with crystals, but I had no way of knowing that at the time. Norma used crystals in all her sessions, and I knew they were something that could enhance not only my Reiki method but also other treatments I did, like massage and reflexology. I also enjoyed connecting with their energy on a personal level by using them in meditations, laying out grids around my house, using them to aid manifestation, and other things.

As soon as I finished my Second-Degree Reiki, I started a Crystal Healing course. The time was right, and I was on a roll of spiritual energy that was carrying me along on a current of cosmic light. I was committed to finding my spiritual alignment and becoming a walking, talking example of it, in every moment of my existence.

As part of the first module in my crystal course, I had to pick a clear quartz crystal to work with, and the one I was drawn to for this exercise was a small quartz point that had occlusions at the base and a phantom right in the centre. I didn't know at the time of picking it that phantoms, because of how they are formed, have had time to put the past into perspective and point towards future growth and evolution. It was where I found myself, especially with regards to my work. I was already on a path as a healer, but up until now, my healing focused on the physical touch of massage and manipulation through other alternative methods. Now that I had completed my Reiki training, I knew I was leaning towards focusing on energy healing techniques, which would uncover the link between the physical and the non-physical. I knew there was a shift going on from my past to my future, and I knew I had to let go and trust my instincts. In doing so, I would allow for these crystals and their magical properties to act as further guides for my highest and greatest good. Little did I know how intense the next part of my journey would be.

As I started to bond with my crystal, it became very apparent that, although I'd seemingly picked *it* from a varied selection on offer, it had in fact chosen me. I was at a turning point in my life, on more levels than I realised, and this crystal would be instrumental in paving the path for me and my future growth. I cleansed it and set the intention for working with it, and then I started to carry the crystal with me in my pocket throughout the day. Instantly, my actions and thoughts became a lot clearer and my focus on them much sharper. At night, I would hold it in my hand as I lay in bed and drift into a meditative state. As soon as I became fully relaxed, I'd feel the quartz melt into my hand and start to travel up through my arm, into my head, back down my other arm and into every cell of my being. It was simultaneously refreshing and peaceful. I would stay in this meditative state until I fell asleep. From the very first night, I had very intense, vivid dreams about people and places from my past. They were things I thought I had made my peace with years ago, but what I came to realise was that although I might have made the peace that I needed to up until that point in time, in order for me to grow and evolve in the direction I was going, I needed to go much deeper.

The next morning when I woke, I opened my curtains, and noticed a seagull hovering in the field in front of my house. I realise that seagull sightings are hardly rare, but a lone baby seagull definitely is, especially where I lived in the Highlands. In fact, I hardly ever saw them on the farm unless a field was ploughed over. Over the next few nights, the faces and places of old continued to visit me in my dream state. Honestly, it wasn't very pleasant, as I was re-visiting a time in my life wrought with fear and darkness. I kept going back to the period of my life when I was 16-18 years old. For me, this was a time when I entered into a relationship that would set the tone of underlying fear for years to come, a time I would have to overcome before I could find my true state of being again, a time when I would no longer simply be a witness to addiction but an addict myself. Those were the two years of my life I lived as a heroin addict.

I was more than a little surprised at this unwelcome resurfacing as a 30-year-old woman, but I knew there was more healing to be done. I needed to work through it and work it out. There was, of course, a greater purpose behind the rehashing of those dark times, as I would soon find out.

A few days had passed since the baby seagull made its appearance, and I was trying not to push for answers. My mind was drawn to the images and emotions that my dreams were stirring up, and although I knew what they were related to, I was unsure of what I needed to do. I've mentioned before that I take full responsibility for all of my actions, and I stand by that. In fact, I cannot stress enough the importance of ownership and accountability when reclaiming your personal power. When you can stand with your head held high and say, "I am responsible for all of my choices in life, both good and bad," then you can no longer be the victim or blame another, and that is truly liberating. Yes, it can be hard to accept that you are the creator of experiences that you would not normally choose, but when you can do this, you also arm yourself with the strength and power needed to turn it around and create what you *do* want. People who know me and my life's story have often said that I was not to blame for becoming a heroin addict, that I was only 16 years old and didn't know better, that I was manipulated into it by a man who was 12 years my senior — my boyfriend. But the truth is, I knew what I was doing. I knew it was wrong, and I knew it was dangerous. I knew I was getting into something that was way over my head. However, as crazy as it may sound, I also knew that this was something I was meant to do — a path I had to go down. What I didn't know is how long this particular chapter would last and how greatly it would impact on my life's journey, on so many levels. The healing would be like cutting into an onion and peeling back each layer, one at a time. But I suppose this is how all healing must take place; we can only work through that which we are ready to let go of, in the timing that is right for our future evolution.

I didn't blame anyone else for my choices but was still unsure about what I needed to do to get complete closure on this subject, so I decided to send Reiki back in time, to see if that would shed any light. And boy oh boy, did it ever. As I sat there in a meditative state, sending Reiki back to that pivotal time in my life, I started to feel an overwhelming sensation of love. It wasn't the kind of love you feel for anyone or anything in particular, but the kind that directed itself and flowed without me having to hold any intention about where it flowed.

First, I needed to send love to myself. I had to absolve myself completely of the guilt I'd carried for so many years for all the pain I'd caused my parents, particularly my dad. I'll never forget the look on his face when I told him I was moving out of the family home and in with a drug dealer — one who happened to be more than a decade older than me. It must have felt like someone was ripping his heart out. No parent in their right mind would approve of such a decision, and it wasn't something that he saw coming. He voiced his concerns, but at no time did he assert his authority or try to enforce anything on me. In spite of all his pain and anguish, he was as strong, diplomatic, and non-judgmental as ever. My father has always allowed my brothers and me the room to become our own people, to make our own mistakes, and to learn from them. Regardless, whenever our broken pieces have needed to be picked up, on account of a foolish decision or poor judgment, he's been there, with arms open wide, ready to help us heal and move on. He is the strongest, most humble man I know. As I've grown older, my respect for him has only increased, and when the time comes for me to face life's challenges with my children, I can only hope that I am as strong and wise as he has always been for me, despite the pain I know I caused him at times.

Next, the love started to flow for the drug-dealing ex — yep, even him — but now it came from a place of understanding and empathy. I could see why he'd become entangled in a life of drugs and all the shit that comes with it. He always saw himself as a victim of life's circumstances. I escaped from this man by climbing out of a window, hiding the key to the door, and then running until my legs couldn't go any more. If it hadn't been for a dear friend who took me in until I could reach my dad, I don't know what would have happened. I still don't know how, but he managed to find me that night anyway. My friend had to call the police, but even that didn't deter him from trying to get to me. It was a frightening and tense situation. Had he been successful in reaching me, I would have been beaten severely. But that was some twenty one years earlier, and I was evolving and growing more every day, so I reached a point where I needed to set myself free from the past pain, on every level, and that meant sending love even to him. I don't know where he is today, but I suspect the same place he was when we were together — both physically and mentally. Nevertheless, I forgive him wholeheartedly. I now know that, like everyone, he was only doing what he knew to do at the time. I see now that his behaviour was governed by his own deep-seated fears and insecurities, and I'm thankful for the lessons I've learned from that time in my life both about myself and addiction, in general. Most importantly, I learned the true meaning of unconditional love.

When I came out of my meditation, I knew exactly what I had to do to put this chapter to rest and be free of its pull once and for all. The meditation was a start, but what I really needed was to go back to my home town and complete the process there. I knew I had to go back and send Reiki to the place and all the people, both known and unknown to me, who may have contributed to my past. This meant finding peace with not just those who had been involved in my life during the two years of my drug addiction but with everyone who was part of my life growing up — directly or indirectly. You see, there are the people and components in situations that we are aware of, who make a big impact, and then there are those who we forget, or possibly don't even realise have played a part or that we've had some kind of effect on. I've not always been the most caring, compassionate person; there will be moments and situations that I've forgotten about — as we all do — so that's why it's important to heal the knowns and unknowns. I knew I had to go home to do just that.

I decided that once I got there, I would go to the top of the biggest dune at the beach. It had been like my second home when I was growing up. It was a place I'd felt connected to all my life, a place of natural cleansing and contemplation. I felt excited I'd pieced together a huge chunk of my past in a way that freed me, and I knew that the action I was about to take would only further my healing and deepen the understanding of the lessons that I had to learn. I was awakening on a whole new level, and as my consciousness expanded, I felt good. It felt right. I knew I was exactly where I needed to be.

The day finally came. It was late autumn and the weather was perfect, cool but surprisingly sunny. I say surprising because, in Scotland, at that time of year, the wind and rain are never far away. That day, there was barely a breath of wind, which was yet another sign that I was following the signposts from Source and that the Universe was backing me up along the way.

Driving down that road, my heart felt like a cup that was full, and the loving energy continued to spill over into every inch of my being. It felt good to connect with the energies of this land again. I'd left a long time ago never thinking I'd return, let alone with so much love in my heart. When I arrived, I did a little detour, driving around the streets that I'd grown up in, past the old houses I'd lived in as a child, reminiscing, and truly enjoying the process. For the first time in years, I felt no pain in my heart as I reconnected with these places. Not all of my memories from there were bad ones, but the final few years spent there had been turbulent and harrowing; it was refreshing to remember the care-free person I had been before my entanglement in the dark world of drug addiction.

As soon as I arrived at the beach, before I even stepped out of the car, I felt my soul lighten. This place had always provided me with the headspace I needed growing up, and it had always been a place of regeneration, so armed with the very piece of phantom quartz crystal that had set this particular healing journey in motion, I set out across the sand towards the big dune known as Tiger Hill. Despite the glorious weather, the beach was very quiet, and that suited me just fine. The last thing I wanted that day was to bump into old friends and acquaintances. This trip was for my spiritual evolution, for me to heal and send healing, so that I could move forward in life and not have the scars of old dictate my vibrational output anymore.

Once at the top, I sat and enjoyed the view as I breathed in deeply the fresh, salty sea air. The happiest of memories began to fill my head, from walks along the beach with my family, to summer parties with my friends, late-night stargazing, and endless summers. Nostalgic tears of happiness began to flow, and with them, feelings of love began to replace the old feelings of dread and fear I had towards this place. I took out my phantom quartz and drew some Reiki symbols over the town. I then focused solely on sending the love, light, and energy to whoever and wherever it needed to go, with the intention of healing from all areas of my past. I cut the energetic chords that bound me to anything, known or unknown to me, that no longer served my highest and greatest good. When I finally came round, almost two hours had passed. And in all that time, not one person had walked by to disturb my peace. I could feel the huge energy shift instantly. I made my way back to my car, thanking the Universe for guiding me to take the inspired action. I felt freer and stronger than I had in a long time.

During my three-hour drive back to the Highlands, I was so full of gratitude, and the thing that I was most grateful for was finally putting myself at the top of my priority list. The inner work that I had started to do was paying off in ways that I could never have imagined, and I knew continuing on this path of self-discovery would only lead me to more alignment, and ultimately, more fulfilment. Energetically, I had closed a door to my past but in a way that was so loving and caring to everyone involved. It helped to strengthen my belief in taking responsibility for my actions because, through this choice, I was empowering myself and not others by playing the victim. And just like that, a door closed. I'd laid my past to rest (or so I thought), and I was excited to see what was next.

The next morning when I awoke and opened my curtains, I noticed that the young seagull that had started this all off a few weeks ago was gone — another sign that I was flowing with my Source energy and allowing myself to follow the guidance of love and light energy.

CHAPTER 5

~

Awakening

I was clocking up so many different experiences and connections to Source and Spirit as I worked on my crystal healing course. Countless guides were presenting themselves to me, offering specific direction about how to work with certain crystals; memories from past lives were all coming thick and fast to help speed up my spiritual evolution. It was as though I was being fast-tracked for something, and frankly, I couldn't get enough. The energy work felt very natural to me, just like when I watched *The Secret* for the first time and felt like I was hearing an eternal truth. The more energy work I did on myself, the more I realised I was returning to my true state of being — an age-old inner truth — and aligning energetically to the Source energy from where we all come.

Over the next months, I became completely engrossed with studying crystals, meditating with them, and receiving guidance from them. I lived and breathed them, in every aspect of my daily life. I was even ingesting their energy by making gem elixirs and charging them with Reiki energy, so that I could become fully saturated with their power. The more I worked with the crystal kingdom, the more in tune I became with it and myself. You see, each crystal is a conscious being, and like people, they all have their unique personality, and through that, the wisdom and guidance that you receive is personal to you. One of the major trace elements found in the human body is silicone, which happens to be the same chemical composition of quartz. Crystals help to shine light on the areas of your life that need healing and balancing, so you can become more of a vibrational match to your higher self and release the old energies that no longer serve your highest and greatest good. They have an uncanny way of digging deep within your soul, sometimes to bring up memories you had forgotten about, sometimes to even heal karmic energy you've been carrying from past lives. When you can hold no expectations of what these fabulous beings can do, their effect on our lives can be nothing less than transformational. Different crystals are coming to the surface now, and their popularity is growing rapidly. They can help humanity transform by raising the collective consciousness, so that we as a whole can live the way we were intended to before coming into our physical bodies, by giving and receiving unconditional love to and from all life. This is our true, natural state of being; we've just forgotten it along the way. It is why so many of us feel disconnection in life. We've forgotten that we are beings of pure love energy.

As the days, weeks, and months went by, I became more of my old self again, only now I was a new and improved version. The more time I spent working on my physical and non-physical energy, the more my inner confidence grew, and the more love and understanding I felt for myself and my life's journey so far. I had reached a plateau of peace with regards to my years of heroin addiction. I was now looking at the wealth of experience I had gained from it, especially in understanding, or trying to understand, my mum's ongoing struggle with alcohol addiction.

As a teenager, I carried a lot of frustration and angst within me because of my mum's drinking. At that age, as my hormones raged and I tried my best to navigate my way through life, I felt a lot of anger towards her. I thought her selfish and unloving sometimes, and I couldn't understand why we (her family) weren't enough for her, why she didn't have more self-restraint when it came to alcohol. She wasn't a happy drunk, either. It made her wallow in misery and dwell on past experiences, which ensured the old vibrational patterns remained active in whichever moment she found herself in. It was always painful memories of sadness and suffering that she held on to, and I could never understand it. But now, I was starting to look at things — at her — with empathy; now my views and insights weren't based on my judgements. Actually, my mum was, and still is, a very loving person. She would go out of her way to help others, when she could, but she was never able to turn that focus and care towards herself.

I was finally starting to see her as a human being, like anyone else, who was scared, vulnerable, self-critical, and had a very low estimate of her own worth. She viewed herself as stupid because she wasn't academic. Throughout my youth, I'd often hear her say, "I'm just stupid, I don't know anything, I'm not good at anything." But it wasn't until now that I was starting to question why she was like this. What had happened to cause her to think so little of herself? Why was she unable to see the strengths that she did have? It didn't make sense; she always had a loving family around her who wanted nothing more than for her to see how loved she was, how much value she gave, and how much she meant to all of us. Still, for some unknown reason, my mum has never been able to see any of these things. She is unable to break down the walls that have been built up over time and let us in to help, and sadly, she is unable to accept responsibility for her actions. I say this completely without judgment, but I've come to realise that not everyone can do this. It was from this observation that I asked myself how I had managed to do the very things she was unable to. I concluded that although I had received the addiction gene from my mum, I had also received my dad's strength of character, self-assuredness, and self-reliance. Ultimately, that helped me overcome my demons. It seems that my mum never had that strength from an outside source to fall back on. My Grandma was also a very delicate soul, and both mum and she were brought up in a time where showing or expressing your feelings was frowned upon. Value was placed on putting on a brave face and just "getting on with it." Unfortunately, mum had filled up her tanks with sadness, hurt, and pain and become trapped in the stories of her past, unable to let them go. From that, her entire life was saturated with the old, negative vibrations, which ultimately led her to become what she believed herself to be.

For the first time in my life, I looked at my mum and thought, "I cannot and will not condemn someone for their weakness." Of course, I would prefer that she was different, but she is who she is. Does that make her any less loving, less of a mum, less worthy of receiving my love? The answer is absolutely not. If it were not for her being who she is, I may not understand true, unconditional love. Through witnessing her lack of confidence and self-worth, it might have been easy for me to get swallowed up by life's bullshit and not be able to value myself as the individual I am. I could have let anger set in and then let it breed into my family, passing on more self-doubt and insecurity, causing more pain and suffering for the future generations of my family. Not me. If anything, I vowed to break this cycle of negative conditioning and promised that I would learn from her. I would not let the pain and suffering that made up most of her life have been in vain. Maybe it was all part of her life's purpose, so that I could learn from her and prevent the mentality of fear and lack from being present in future generations. You see, sometimes the gifts we're given in life don't always come packaged with a fancy bow; sometimes, they're disguised from our immediate view because we're so used to seeing them as something we don't want. Every day, I can see the pain and torment that my mother goes through. But her being who she is has given me one of the greatest gifts I could ever have asked for. I've gained the perspective and understanding that will allow me to live my life differently, to not let fear shape my life, to actively encourage open communication, and work through the emotions we all experience, without shame. Her suffering forced me to seek out a life of alignment and balance that I can pass on to my family, my friends, my clients, and to everyone who encounters me. It has allowed me to find a path in which I can live from a place of genuine, unconditional love, and for me, that is a priceless gift that I believe we should all have access to.

My newfound perspective towards mum and her struggles opened me up to a whole new way of looking at life. Nothing is ever as straight forward or one sided as it appears. The crystals were giving me fresh eyes to view things through, and they were pushing the limits and boundaries that I'd lived my life with thus far. This perception and understanding would only continue to grow over time and feed my hunger to learn more, to connect more, and to find alignment with Source on an even more profound level.

Although I was doing countless meditation exercises with my crystals, and Reiki on myself most days, I also started to do a body scanning exercise at night in bed. It's a very simple relaxation technique where you start at your feet and work up to the top of your head. For the first two weeks or so, I wouldn't make it past my hips before I fell asleep, but I persevered with it, and it wasn't long before I would reach my crown, and then, after two to three months, I was drifting off on some other-worldly experiences. You see, like with all things in life, you get out what you put in. At no point did I do these exercises thinking I'd have an out-of-body experience, astral project, or make contact with a certain guide or being. I did these meditations and other relaxation techniques because I enjoyed them and how I felt during and afterwards. I was gaining more clarity in every aspect of my life, and through that, I was becoming more empowered as I was acting from a place of love. Over time though, with repeated practise of these techniques, I was receiving more input from Source, and when things happened, like outer body experiences, or my guides meeting up with me during meditations, I loved it. I saw it as a reward from Source for continually putting in the effort and the practice. My Reiki Guide, Black Elk, seemed to respond to me very clearly and enthusiastically when I was regular with my efforts. It was during these night-time relaxation techniques that he would appear and take me away.

One night, as I lay in bed doing my centring and grounding, I was visualising a golden ball of light at my centre, and although I knew instantly that it felt different, I continued with my focus. Suddenly, the golden ball of light grew so rapidly in size, it was filling the entire room. In my mind's eye, a campfire appeared, and as I focused on it, I realised I was standing in a forest, and in the distance was another campfire. Staring intently at it, I took one enormous leap, until I was standing next it. Out of nowhere, another fire appeared in the distance, and I leaped toward that one, then another and another. This fire hopping happened another five or six times until I found myself outside a tepee. As soon as I saw it, I knew Black Elk had summoned me.

I love that our encounters are always on his terms because it affirms that I've earned my 'upgrade' and evolved to my next energetic level. It means that my energy has grown all it can, which entitles me to another energetic download, to increase my awareness and consciousness to Universal energy. This, in turn, allows me to evolve on every level, especially with the amount of Source energy I can channel, whether it be for myself or others, during a healing session. From this comes a heightened level of understanding. I gain more clarity through my thoughts and intuition. It is exciting, and it's part of the reason I strive to find more alignment and balance in life. It leads to me experiencing life with more love and more joy — the way it is meant to be experienced. I walked into the tepee, and I was looking all around me trying to take in as much as I could. I could hear Black Elk laughing as he said, "I appreciate your willingness to learn and to saturate yourself with as much information as possible, but you won't be here long enough to take in all of the surroundings." There was a huge, wooden, Native American peace pipe lying next to me, and he signalled for me to pick up the end and place it to my mouth. The pipe was so big that he had to walk to the other end to light it. As he did, he instructed me to inhale, which I did. I immediately became light-headed; I dropped the pipe and started to fall to the left. As I fell, I noticed him walking quickly behind me ready to catch me, and just as my head made contact with his hands, I woke up to find that it was morning, and I was at home in my bed.

What was supposed to be a half-hour meditation had turned into an epic, six-hour astral projection session! The reason I know it wasn't just a dream is that I was still in my meditation position, with the crystals I'd placed on my body exactly where I'd left them. Had I been asleep, I would have rolled over. I knew I'd just received another initiation from Black Elk, which meant I had levelled up again. When you start to work with Reiki energy, at first, it's like a trickle — albeit a powerful one — and the more you work with it, the more you open up. And when you're consistent in your practice and application of it, your guides come in to take you to the next level; at least, that's how it works with me. Ever since the beginning, Black Elk has waited to see my level of commitment before appearing with new guidance and awareness, so needless to say, I was excited and buzzing from the experience, while simultaneously feeling honoured and humbled that this great spirit was still there working with me and my energy — another sign that I was indeed following my life's true path.

Another night, after going to bed and performing the technique, the last thing I remember is holding onto the focus of my crown chakra before I suddenly sat upright in bed with a jolt. I could hear loud noises that are, even now, difficult to describe accurately. The best I can do is to say they were something like a dull but heavy groaning sound, almost as though there was machinery work going on right outside my window. I jumped out of bed, and although it was already daylight, it was still only around 4 or 5 am. I couldn't see anything outside my bedroom window, certainly no construction, so I walked through the house to look out from the other rooms, but still I could see nothing. I did notice that the volume of the noise remained the same, even as I walked from room to room. I climbed back into bed and sat for a few moments before realising that the mysterious sound was actually coming from me. Actually, it was coming from inside my head. At first, it was quite a startling realisation, scary even, so I quickly took control of my thoughts by taking a deep, steady breath in and out through my nose. As I did this, I was able to separate all of the different sounds, so that they weren't so overwhelming, and it was at this point that it dawned on me. Through being able to control the sound of the energies by focusing on the different pitches — and a deep inner knowing in my gut — I could hear my body's energies! I was overwhelmed with emotion and cried with happiness. In that moment, I felt a whole connection to oneness and to Universal energy and Source. I also knew that if I had tried to consciously make this happen, it never would have, but by letting go and holding no expectation of the technique, other than enjoying the feeling of it, I was able to experience something that I never thought I would.

I lingered in bed a while longer, enjoying the intoxicating sounds and sensations that were moving through my being, just allowing them to be. They eventually began to quieten, but for the rest of the day I walked about hearing everything as though I had new ears. My sense of hearing became so amplified that I saw this as another sign from Source that my journey and my commitment to it were leading me to live a life of greater alignment and joy. The best part about it was that my commitment was effortless. It was enjoyable and never felt like a chore. When I choose to do the things that help me to stay aligned and focused, my life flows so much better, and this was apparent to me from the very beginning of this journey. Of course, there are days when I don't get everything done, and that's OK. If I miss a yoga session, or I meditate a little bit later in the day, I don't beat myself up about it because my priority is feeling good. When things arise in life that call for my schedule to change for a few days, I try to adapt. I am OK with missing days or practice sessions when time gets the better of me because I am safe in the knowledge that falling back into old habits is not an option. It's not an option because I know that my life flows the way I want it to when I do my regular practices. I know that it's these things that keep me aligned. I know how I feel when they're not part of my regular routine, and I simply cannot and will not go back to feeling lost and disconnected ever again. I have learned that making myself a conscious priority makes me perform at my optimum. So, beating myself up if I miss a session or two is a direct contradiction to what alignment and feeling good is all about. When a continued effort is made, then empowerment becomes the norm, and once you've sampled that feeling in your life, you'll never want to be without it.

CHAPTER 6

~

A Time for Change

Life was flowing so well, or rather, I was flowing so well! Through all the daily practices, my journey of self-discovery, and connecting the puzzle pieces to make sense of my life so far, I finally understood the concept of *going with the flow*. I was beginning to let go of the reigns of control, and by that, I mean I wasn't trying to dictate exactly how my life and the components in it should pan out. There was now room for play, which had been missing for so long. I was beginning to see that by focusing too much on how things *should* materialise, I would inadvertently reject the very thing I was trying to attract. Letting go finally made sense. You can only let go when you have a deep sense of knowing that things will work out the way you want because that's how and where you're shaping your energy. That is the vibration that you're sending out. Until we can do that, our faith in the energy of the Universe, and ultimately, in ourselves, is weakened. This means that by not letting go, we are still operating from a place of fear that we're not enough and repeating the story of unworthiness that we tell ourselves when, in fact, nothing could be further from the truth.

We are all worthy, powerful beings; we've just forgotten our true value. But by aligning ourselves energetically with our mind, body, and spirit, we can not only become connected with our true value but live a life of empowerment in everything we do. Once the awareness of what we are capable of really sinks in, ideas move beyond simply being a dream or a fantasy to reality. Our emotions shift from hoping to knowing, and believe me when I say, *that* shift in perception is a huge game changer!

It had been nearly two years since I first started to shift my mindset and work on daily energy alignment. I had become comfortable with how life was moving and how I was interacting with it all. I began to think about how I wanted to shape my life, how I wanted to live, and the different things I wanted to do. I was thinking about the endless possibilities that awaited me with my newfound freedom of thinking and being. So, I started to ask myself questions like, "What would my ideal life look like? Where would I like to see myself working and living? What would be exciting for me?" These questions helped me to form the image of a setting I could fill with the colours of my choosing. I was coming to terms with the truth that we are all the creators of our life's story, and that by using our energies properly, we could realise all of our wildest fantasies. This pumped me up and made me feel ready to take on anything!

For the next few weeks, I let the questions roll around inside my head without focusing too much on them. I wanted the ideas to evolve naturally, without over thinking; I had learned by now that overthinking can kill dreams before they've even had a chance to take off. I loved my job, and I was good at it, but I was already getting fed up with the beauty side of it. I had been learning and working more with energies, and I felt that the time for a change was approaching. I was preparing myself for that change, so I decided to focus more on massage and reflexology — the parts of my work that I loved most. I used these as starting points to introduce people to energy healing. As time went by, I was doing more and more Reiki, and even when I had massage clients, the Reiki was finding its way into the sessions. I would start to feel it flow whenever it was needed (and that was often), which led to my massage treatments changing to allow for the practice of more Reiki. At the end of those sessions, I would perform energy traces and then add in a chakra balancing until people were able to recognise their own energy flows and were really feeling the benefits for themselves. This newfound ability would often have a flow-on effect into other areas of my clients' lives. It didn't take long for me to realise the direction that I wanted to take with my work, but it would take a little longer to fine tune it.

I concluded that I wanted to help people become more energetically aligned and aware of how that alignment spanned through all aspects of their life. At that point in my life, and my career, massage played an important role in that it was, among other things, a good starting point for introducing people to energy healing work as it complemented a massage session naturally and easily. I was also beginning to feel like I needed a change of scenery and that I would like to travel more, so these factors started to seep into my consciousness and into my thought patterns about where my life and career may go. I wanted to be in an environment of creativity, while also being able to help others become the best version of themselves. I also wanted to meet new and exciting people in places that would be different from the norm. I needed to expand my world, and I suppose I was ready for the energy of new places and people to be part of my life. I was beginning to outgrow my surroundings, and although I was still perfectly happy where I was, I had just about done all I could do from there. It was likely the Highlands would remain my base for a while, but I needed to travel further afield; I needed to discover where my "home" was, and to do that, I had to start exploring.

Subconsciously, I was preparing myself to begin a new chapter of expansion, but as always, if too much were to have been revealed to me at the time, I would probably have retreated in fear. So, I put my new intention out to the Universe and carried on with what I'd been doing, knowing that the Universe would deliver at the perfect time, as long as I didn't self-sabotage and hinder the delivery. The only way to do that was to continue with my own energy work and keep using the tools and techniques that had helped me stay on the path to alignment thus far. That would then highlight the signs given to me by Source to keep me on that path, keep me living joyfully, and highlight my true calling.

My heart was pulling me in the direction of energy work, but much of my bread and butter work was still firmly anchored in the beauty side. After all, I was good at it, and although I wanted to get away from those types of treatments, I knew they were still serving a purpose and that I needed to be grateful for the things I had in my life that were allowing me to have and keep my freedom. Therefore, instead of losing interest, I remained in a state of gratitude for my abilities and for the clients I already had. I trusted that by holding on to my intention for positive growth and change, the opportunities I truly sought would present themselves at the right time.

One day, the idea came to me that providing massage treatments at concerts and music festivals for the performing artists would be a fun environment for me to work in. I knew of some festivals and venues in the Highlands that could use my services, so I got to work on creating a small package that would showcase and explain what I had to offer. I had a few connections in the music industry, so I contacted them and got names and details of people I could reach out to for the purpose of promoting myself. I felt this was a good idea, and I believed in my abilities, but I wasn't completely sure that it would be successful. Although I had come a long way in changing my mindset, this was new, uncharted territory; I was stepping outside my comfort zone and embarking on a new challenge, so it was inevitable that I was going to come up against some self-doubt and reunite with some old paradigms regarding my capabilities. As soon as the fear began to set in, I did what I needed to do to get my mind back on track and remind myself that I was worthy of my desires and that if I wanted to do something, the only person preventing it from happening would be me. It was at that point that I decided to enlist the help of a mentor. We all need someone to be accountable to for our actions because, left to our own devices, it becomes all too easy to make up excuses and put off the action steps that we know we need to take, thereby keeping our goals entrapped in the 'fantasy' realm. But, when we have someone other than ourselves to call us out on our bullshit, someone who will say, "There's no real reason why you can't make a start on those plans," then we are more likely to succeed.

I had never had an official coach or mentor before, but I was still studying and furthering my education with energy alignment, so I did have my Reiki Master to turn to for advice, and I had a determination to prove to myself that I had what it took to walk my talk. I had proof in my life already of what could happen when I took inspired action. I wanted to take responsibility for my actions, or lack of, so this helped to fuel my inner fire. In hindsight, it was through my personal development work that I knew I had what it took to coach and serve others. Had I not done things this way, I might have never developed that deep knowing and faith in myself and my abilities. This time in my life was me laying the foundations for how I would not only live my life but also help others to identify how they want to live theirs. Piece by piece, the puzzle was fitting together to create a picture more stunning and magical than I could have ever imagined. I could feel it beginning to come together, although it would be years from that point that I would see how the pieces would reveal themselves.

Without changing too much, except for how I saw myself during meditations and visualisations to do with my career, things started to change. I started getting more massage clients and fewer beauty clients. I was getting more private hire work from high-end hotels and private estates which meant I was hiring myself and my services out for day rates rather than filling up my day with numerous clients at different locations. There was more travel further afield, and in the process, I was meeting people from very different backgrounds. I was getting the changes I had been asking for, although they were manifesting in a different form than I'd imagined. This is why it is so important when trying to manifest anything that you keep an open mind and try not to be too precise about how it will materialise. In days gone by, I would have found fault with how things were turning out because it wasn't going exactly how I had planned it in my mind, but I could see the Universe was, in fact, delivering to me the experiences and situations that I was asking for, and it was doing it in a way that I was able to flow with. It wasn't causing me to become overwhelmed and then push it away. I put my trust in it, and as a result, more opportunities came into my life. So many of my clients would tell me of their own journeys and experiences of going from scepticism and doubt to putting their faith in the Universe, only to have it deliver exactly what they wanted all along. The signs would pour in from everywhere to keep me focused, to keep my belief strong, and I made sure to be thankful and express my gratitude for them. The people that I was attracting through my work were matching the vibration that I was sending out, and for me, that was further proof that the law of attraction was and always is working.

Then, one day, I got an email from the production company that was in charge of organising a music festival on the outskirts of Inverness, saying that they would love to have me there to provide massage for the performing artists backstage. I was over the moon! A very specific dream of mine was about to be realised, so I got to work with increasing my vibe even more so that I could flow with this new opportunity rather than become swept away by the excitement of it all. I allowed myself to feel the excitement, but I had planted a seed of an idea, and with my trust, the Universe had delivered. So now, I wanted to make the most of this opportunity. I meditated, visualised, and decided on the best way to use the tools and knowledge that I had gathered so far for aligning energetically with it for the highest and greatest good. It was fun to let my imagination run wild and put my energy into situations that made me feel good. It was fun and exciting to acknowledge that through identifying with my real heart's desires, I could manifest the reality that I chose. And if it could work with this, it could be done with any other loving desire.

A few weeks passed, and the time came for me to work backstage at my first music festival. I was excited but nervous, and I had to work at keeping my energies grounded so as not to become overwhelmed. I kept reminding myself to enjoy the experience, to savour each moment, and to not hold any expectation about it as that would be a sure way to throw contrast into the mix and undo all of the positive work I had put in. After all, it's quite easy to go back into old patterns of thought and action and to ruin the experience of the moment. Change can be uncomfortable, but instead of allowing the fear to set in, we need to remind ourselves that once we've faced our fear about the change, it is almost never as bad as we make it out to be. The unknown can be fun, if we go with the flow and take it one step at a time, so that's what I did for the next three days. I held no expectation and went with the flow.

It was a very enjoyable three days. I was already comfortable being around celebrities — I'd had a few as clients over the years — so I was aware of the demands and expectations of some of them, and even if I did feel star struck on the inside, I was well-rehearsed at not letting it show and remaining professional at all times. I reminded myself that, like me, they were just people who breathe in the same air and use the toilet same as we all do! Without this insight, it would be easy for things to spiral out of control, or feel out of your depth in situations, but if we strip it all back to basics, it's easier to navigate our way through. Once we've navigated our way through one new situation, we create the vibration in our energy to welcome in more new, wonderful experiences that will add to our growth and alignment with Source.

I left the music festival with the knowledge that I would be asked back again the following year, which was music to my ears and soul. I'd met so many people, all of whom were lovely and very appreciative of the services I'd provided, so all in all, it was a very productive and enjoyable experience. I had manifested a dream quite quickly with very little action required, and it felt good to know that my practices and new belief systems were indeed helping me align with my higher self, and I knew this was a continuation and deepening of the connection that we all hold to the energies of creation. And it felt amazing!

Over the summer, I continued to get more massage work and more clients that wanted to hire me, sometimes for days at a time, which meant I no longer needed to take on any beauty work. It was yet another step in the right direction to how I wanted things to play out. There was abundance in every area of my life, which had been missing for so long. I was enjoying time away with my friends, nights out, fine dining, and real, meaningful relationships, though not in the romantic sense. I hadn't been looking for romance; frankly, I'd been so busy and so happy building the relationship with myself that attracting someone on an intimate level had taken a back seat. There was no room in my mind or my energy for romance, and if I had attracted someone, it would have been the wrong person, at the wrong time, again! And this was something that I wanted to avoid at all costs. However, I was starting to think along the lines that it would be nice to have someone to share that type of connection with, but this time, I knew I wouldn't settle for someone whose energy wasn't a match to who I'd become. I would not sacrifice my highest and greatest good anymore because I knew I was enough for me. I didn't need someone else to make me feel complete, but I wanted someone that would enhance my existence, someone I could grow with but who could also challenge me and support me energetically. I never paid too much attention to this, but as the Universe is responding to our energy more than our thoughts, I guess that this energetic output coming from me was starting to put things in motion (behind the scenes, anyway). And pretty soon, there would be more signs in my physical reality that would be hard for me to ignore.

CHAPTER 7

~

Mating Season

Two very dear friends of mine announced that they were getting married, and it was going to be fantastic. Robert, who I'd worked with and grown close to when I first moved up to Dornoch, was now the manager at The Torridon House Hotel. He and his partner Bruce had set a date for February of the following year, and it was to be a weekend-long event in Torridon — a lovely, small village in the Northwest Highlands. To this day, their wedding is still one of the best I've been to. It's always nice to celebrate the love between two people, especially when they're as loving and caring as Robert and Bruce.

The weekend was fun filled from beginning to end, in one of the most beautiful settings that Scotland has to offer, with some of the nicest people I've had the pleasure of meeting. I attended the wedding by myself as there was no room for plus ones with the limited numbers the hotel could accommodate. Not having a partner to go with might have put some people off, but I didn't mind. I was in such a great place physically, mentally, and emotionally, my two very close friends were getting married, and I knew several of the other guests that would be attending the wedding.

One of the most amazing moments from their special day for me was when the wedding rings were passed around. It was a humanist wedding — or civil ceremony as it's called in some parts of the world — and before they presented each other with the wedding bands, everyone got to hold them and silently say a blessing or prayer for good luck. When it was my turn to hold the rings, I opened my Reiki channel, drew the power symbol over both rings and then filled them with love, and the light energy of Reiki for the couple's highest and greatest good. After the ceremony, all the guests had gathered for some pre-dinner drinks and canapés, and I was chatting to Robert and Bruce. Bruce asked me what I had done to the wedding rings (Bruce is very intuitive and can see auras, but he doesn't do anything involving energy work). I smiled and asked why. He replied by saying that when Robert put the ring on his finger, he could see a noticeably clear symbol; he described it as being similar to a treble clef. When I told them I had blessed the rings with Reiki and drew over them the power symbols, he stated excitedly, "I knew it! I knew that was you!" Now, in case you're wondering, there was no way either of them could have seen me and what I was doing; I had been sitting right at the back of the room, and they were chatting away with the lady who was conducting the ceremony at the time. What a beautiful moment of connection and alignment, not only with Robert and Bruce but with everything, with all energy. I saw this as yet another sign from the Universe that I was indeed on my path, and I was following the guidance given to me in the right manner.

At the end of that glorious weekend, just before I left, I signed the guest book. I wrote some words and drew the symbol I had placed over the rings. Bruce came over and said, "That's it, that's the symbol I saw!" Hearing that filled my heart with such joy. I just love those moments when we get presented with situations and experiences that we know are true, but there is no way on earth you can explain how. You see, miracles do happen all the time. The Universe is always aware of you and is always responding directly to your energy with perfection and wonder, all at the same time. Moments like this keep me inspired, keep my faith strong, and prove to me that what matters the most is the energetic connections we have. Because everything is energy, and all energy is one.

I'll never forget the day I arrived home after the wedding. It was late February, and it was cold! There had been some snow, and there was a hard frost — the kind that clings to the blades of grass — covering them in a layer of velvety ice crystals that crunched underfoot as you walked over them. It was a beautiful day, the sun was shining, and the icy cold air which took your breath away was very still. As I pulled up in front of my house, I walked over to the burn that flowed down alongside my garden. The most beautiful icicles had formed on the stones and pebbles that were in the flowing water and on some of the wild grass that draped over from the banks at the side of the burn. I have never seen icicles like them. They looked like alien creatures, crystal clear and large, and there were so many! I was excited by what I saw, and right then and there I decided that I would wrap up nice and warm and spend some time down by the burn (a Scottish term for a small stream), enjoying Mother Nature's show of beauty and wonder that she'd put on for me. I unpacked my stuff from the car, got a scarf and my camera from inside and then, armed with a thick blanket to sit on, I made my way down the small grassy bank and got comfortable. I loved my burn; the running water has always had an instant calming effect on me. I loved the sounds and the different shapes that the water makes as it travels downstream, not to mention it was my favourite place to cleanse my crystals. It was a small burn, but it was always so full of life. In the spring and summer there would be wildflowers growing, dragonflies, butterflies and birds, and the same pair of ducks had been coming back there for the last few years. It really did have a magical feel to it, and that day was no exception.

It must have been the best part of three hours I spent there that day, just enjoying the moment and the icicles. I took some photos and meditated, and as I did, I got the feeling that someone was about to enter my life soon. As I made my way back up from the burn to my house, a very large male pheasant appeared from under one of the bushes in my garden and started screaming. I was a bit taken aback but laughed; he seemed very boisterous and bold for a pheasant. I spoke to him (I speak to a lot of birds), and then I went back into my house and thought no more about it. The next morning, I was awoken by the pheasant and his screams again. I looked out of my window, and there he was, sitting just underneath the bush where he'd been the day before. He screamed for about ten to fifteen minutes and walked around in a circle before going back into the bush. My attention turned to a male partridge clucking about on the grass. I'd never seen a partridge in my garden, and he too looked like he was making himself at home, so I got some wild bird seed and put it outside next to where the partridge was walking and some more next to the bush where the pheasant was. I could see the pheasant had taken up residence by the bed he'd built under the bush. Now the screaming made sense; it was a mating call.

A few days passed, and still the pheasant and partridge remained in my garden. I was feeding them every day and enjoying their beauty and their company, and even the pheasant's screaming first thing in the morning became a source of joy. He was so loud and so persistent it made me laugh when I heard him. Besides, I was rooting for him to find his mate — to have that sense of fulfilment through the natural yearning that he had within. It was coming up to the end of February, my work was a little quieter, but I didn't mind; it gave me time to focus on my inner being, my alignment, and where I wanted to focus my energies. The cool, sunny days were telling my soul that spring was just around the corner, that it would soon be time for nature to come out of its slumber and begin the process of rebirth. Summer is my favourite time of the year, but the excitement I feel just as spring is about to kick into action gets me all fired up inside. I know that, like all things in nature, I am about to come alive again after the period of hibernation and reflection that winter gifts us each year. And this year, I could feel a big change was about to come. I didn't know how this change would take form in my life, and by this time I knew I didn't need to know, I just had to hold onto the excited anticipation that I felt deep within, and whatever was coming would come into full bloom at exactly the right time.

One night, after a full day of being immersed in my crystal healing course, I came out of a deep meditation. I'd been focusing on clearing and balancing my chakras through different methods of using crystals and also grid work (when you lay out crystals at different points around you, or a space). The grid of crystals intensifies the energies and makes for a more powerful healing session, which I found incredibly exciting. Grids amplify the energies of everything, and with some deliberate intentions set into the crystals as they're laid out, it creates more focus and a deeper level of understanding of yourself, your energy, and how that relates to your everyday life. My attention had been brought to subconscious feelings of being unworthy of fully receiving my dreams and desires, which boiled down to a lack of self-love. Even my Reiki guide, Black Elk, made an appearance to remind me that we are all the same, and we all deserve for our dreams and desires to reach fruition; the only one that prevents this from happening is us. This made me think deeply about where and when this seed of doubt had been planted. I couldn't recall anyone in my life actually saying that I was undeserving of anything, but as I connected with the emotion, I realised that I projected this thought from myself onto others. By this I mean that I convinced myself that others were thinking I was unworthy — my ego was playing tricks on me — and I took those made up thoughts to be truth. I started making extra effort to remind myself that I am loved, that I am worthy of all my desires no matter what they might be, to not judge myself or others, and to justify my dreams to no one, not even myself. Judgment and the seeking of approval for one's dreams are sure fire ways to create resistance toward them and to ensure that they never come to pass. As I sat up and came round after my meditation, I looked out of my upstairs window across at the farm and the beautiful dusk sky as the sun set. I noticed a bird flying straight toward me. It was some distance away, but I could tell that it was a rarely sighted bird of substantial size. As it neared, I wondered if it might be an albatross but couldn't quite believe it as they were so rare in that part of Scotland. And as it flew right over my bedroom window with its legs hanging low, I realised it was in fact a beautiful, graceful heron. I knew at once that the heron was a sign of things to come.

Later that week, I was gathered in my living room with some good friends, watching films and enjoying each other's company. It was still daylight outside when something caught my eye through the window. I stood up to get a proper look, and to my surprise, a heron was standing in the garden looking right at me through the window. I smiled, knowing there was meaning behind this, and this was the heron's second visit in as many days. Needless to say, I was curious to know what was coming next.

The heron continued to look right at me, bowed and then flew away. I sat back down in my seat, acknowledging that I'd received a message from Source, even though that message was not yet clear. As I mulled over this, I was left with a distinct feeling that someone new was about to come into my life. Initially, I thought that it probably had to do with my work, such as a new contact or client that would have some effect on my overall career direction. As I pondered all of these thoughts and scenarios, I did my best to contain them and remind myself that I didn't need to figure out all the details; they would soon be revealed to me. The heron is a symbol of patience, you see. When hunting for food, the heron will often sit still in the same position for hours at a time, just waiting for a fish to appear in the right spot. And my heron was telling me that I too needed to be patient, and I would get my fish, so to speak.

A week or so passed, and my resident pheasant remained in his bush, calling out multiple times a day for a mate. I was beginning to wonder how long he was going to have to wait before his calls would bear fruit. The partridge had gone, I hadn't seen him for a few days, and I wondered where he was. Had he gone off to find a mate? And then it dawned on me: the pheasant, the partridge, and I'm pretty sure the heron too, were all male birds. The something, or someone rather, who was about to come into my life was going to be a man. As I made my way outside to top up the birdseed for Mr pheasant, there was the heron, bathing in the burn by the side of my house. He was definitely a male; I could

69

tell by the size of him and by how my energy felt while going over the question in my mind. It was intriguing, even though I wasn't actively on the lookout for a romantic partner. While there were times when I thought it would be nice to have someone special to share things with, and to share intimacy with, I didn't need a man to fulfil me. I'd already promised myself that no man would enter into the sphere of my world again unless he was truly supportive, understanding, and so comfortable and sure of himself that he never felt the need to try and change me. I could provide all that I needed in life, including the right kind of love for myself, but it felt like a romantic partner was heading my way, and the pheasant seemed to be the major sign. I acknowledged it and said that I was excited to see what the Universe had in store for me and left it at that.

A few more days had passed when a couple of female pheasants started to hang about in the field across from the burn, much to the delight of my male resident. There were many male courting shows on display, and they must have impressed the ladies because, the next day, Mr pheasant was nowhere to be seen. His patience had been rewarded, and now he was off to fulfil the next part of his destiny by fathering some chicks and keeping the circle of life turning. The days passed, and my signs seemed to stop. No one seemed to be appearing in my life, but I trusted that those signs had happened for a reason and something would show up eventually. I put it to one side and got on with life, studying, working, and enjoying the person I'd become.

My 31st birthday had passed, and I was feeling very confident and happy with my life. I felt more connected to my higher self and purpose than ever. Spring arrived, and with it the longer days. There were lambs in the fields and daffodils displaying their golden trumpets all over the countryside. There was a feeling of growth and expansion in the air, and I was relishing it. One night in April, I was in the middle of a spring clean when I came across a St Christopher necklace that I was gifted when I was fifteen years old. As soon as I held it, memories of a very dear, old friend of mine, Glen Morrice, came flooding back. Glen and I had dated when we were younger, and if I'm honest, he was someone who popped into my mind from time to time. I liked Glen — a lot. When we were together, it was easy and fun. But we were young, and neither of us had developed ease of communication about how we truly felt about each other. Glen had gifted me the St Christopher necklace, though at the time I never realised just how significant this gift was. Had I known the importance of it when I received it, life could have played out in a whole different way, so I now realise that the significance of that necklace was lost on me for a reason back then. I was pleased to find it, and as I held it, I enjoyed reminiscing and wondering where Glen was and what he was doing now. After some time, I put the necklace back into the box and carried on with my spring clear out.

Two weeks had passed exactly to the day since I'd found my St Christopher, and when I turned on my laptop and logged in to Facebook, there was a friend request from none other than

Glen Morrice! Excitement consumed me from the inside out. I accepted the request straight away, and within minutes I received a message from him. He asked how I was and where I was living. It had been fifteen years since I had last seen him. I had left my home town and very rarely went back to visit, so I knew nothing of his life or what he'd been up to all these years. He told me that he was still living in the same house, and even more surprising, he lived there alone. So many memories came flooding back. I'd spent many a day and night in that house, and it was there that he gifted me the St Christopher's necklace. I remembered that night so clearly, and I could feel all the emotions wash over and through me. It was nice, but I was also surprised by the intensity of the emotions that I was feeling. Was this the man who was about to enter my life? It couldn't be, I thought, not Glen. He was from a place and time in my life that I never thought I would return to, yet it felt so good to be in contact with him again. The communication with him was resonating with me at a soul level, and I liked it. We exchanged quite a few messages every day over the next week or so. It was fun, and I was enjoying receiving some flirty male attention. After all, it had been a long time since I'd had that in my life.

Glen was offshore at the time, working on the oil rigs, and was due to come home soon. I casually invited him to come and visit. I wasn't looking for a serious relationship at that point in my life, and in my mind, I thought that we could maybe meet up from time to time and enjoy each other's company without any strings attached. I was focused on my career, and he was newly single again. It seemed the perfect situation for some carefree fun. He accepted my invitation, and we arranged for him to come and visit by train. I would pick him up, we'd have a good time, and then go our separate ways until the next time. I had it all figured out and this arrangement suited me perfectly.

It was on the 9th May 2010 that Glen came up to see me. I was excited but there was not one bit of me that thought this could be anything serious. My best friend, Theresa, even asked me the night before he came, "So this Glen, is he someone that could distract you from your focus?" to which I replied, "No, absolutely not! I mean don't get me wrong, he's a really nice guy, but this will just be a bit of fun, nothing serious!" Famous last words.

Glen got the train in to Inverness. I lived about forty-five minutes away, and as I was driving to pick him up, a huge flood of panic came over me. My heart started beating fast, my palms were sweaty, and I kept thinking to myself, "What on earth am I doing?" It had been so easy and natural chatting on the phone, just like old times. We laughed as he teased me about having lost my broad Doric accent and how posh I sounded. It had been light-hearted and fun, but now I was going to meet him again. What would I say? What was he going to be like? I hadn't ever experienced nerves like it before, and I had to pull over to the side of the road and phone Theresa to calm me down, which she did, but I was still sick with nerves.

The journey there was easy, and everything seemed to be going my way — I even got a parking space right outside the front of the train station, which hardly ever happens. I was aware of the ease, and I knew I was in my flow, aligned with my higher self. This was all meant to be, I kept telling myself, as I stood nervously waiting for the train to pull up into the station. But I still felt like an awkward teenager again, all sweaty palms and shuffling feet, and this made me laugh because I was only a teenager the last time we met. And then, there he was, beaming that big, infectious smile of his as he walked towards me. My heart skipped a beat with excitement, but there was also a feeling of safety and comfort washing over me. As I watched him coming towards me, it was as though only a week had passed since we last met. There was a familiarity in the energy between us; it was natural, flowed easily, and before I knew it, he had his arms wrapped around me, embracing me tightly. The best way I can describe the feeling of that moment is that it felt like coming home. He felt like home — the embrace my higher self had been assuring me did exist. It was one of the most beautiful feelings of connection that I've ever felt with someone and, just like that, all of the nerves, the sweaty palms, and insecurities vanished. Even now, I can feel it all over again and it evokes the same tears of joy and the deep inner knowing that true love does exist and always did. It had simply been waiting for the right time to present itself to us. The conversation between us flowed easily and naturally, and I smiled from ear to ear. I was happy, and this was going to be a good weekend of fun — just what I needed to re-charge and re-fresh my 'feminine'— and then, afterwards, I would get back to focusing on me and my future. I was going to enjoy each moment and allow the feelings of joy and happiness to saturate my being fully.

A young me, age 16, about 6 months before
I became addicted to heroin.

Me and my brother Alec at his wedding

Me and my other brother Chris. I was heavily addicted to
heroin when these pictures were taken.

Year 2000; me, just after finishing college and starting work full-
time at Skibo; this was the night I met Robert.

Graduation photo September, 2000

Skibo Castle, home to Andrew Carnegie and the beginning of
my love affair with the Highlands of Scotland.

Theresa and I at a Christmas party

2011; Our mad night in Malaga, Spain.

2007; Christmas night out — the smile hides how very unhappy I was at home. This was the beginning of the end of my relationship at the time.

One of the picturesque views on the drive to Norma's, taken on a little humpback bridge in Ardgay.

A panoramic view of Fraserburgh beach, taken from
the top of Tiger Hill

Looking across Fraserburgh beach with tiger
Hill in the distance.

Me at Cullykhan bay. A few miles from Fraserburgh,
after I had gone back to send healing to my past in 2009.

Robert and Bruce's wedding and the moment when Bruce saw the
Reiki symbol I blessed the rings with.

The happy, newlywed couple.

Me at Robert and Bruce's wedding, feeling empowered and free, and slowly getting back to being a blonde!

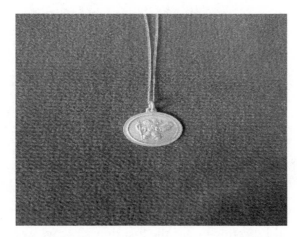

The St Christopher I got from Glen when I was a teenager;

The pheasant that took up residence in my garden as
a sign that a man was about to enter my life.

Glen and I meeting up for the first time since we were young.

2011, Glen and I at the
"Pirates Graveyard" in Gamrie, a few miles from Fraserburgh.

2012, Glen and I with our dear friends, Theresa and Xavier,
during one of our rambles over to the West Coast of Scotland;

Glen and Xavier, who formed a very strong
bromance straight away.

Theresa and I laughing at ourselves! Never a dull moment when we are together.

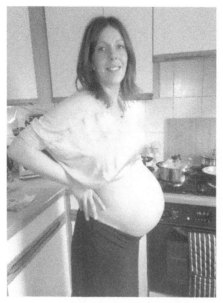

A very pregnant me! I loved my pregnancy.

Me with Leo when he was about 3 days old.

My mam and dad.

September 2014: our wedding day.
Dad, me, Glen, and mam.

April, 2015: The house Glen and I manifested with Bob Proctor's abundance meditation.

My dear friend and Coach, Suzana Mihajlovic

My 40th birthday celebrations.

Enjoying a drop in Barcelona — the trip was my 40th birthday present from Glen.

Norma, my beautiful friend and Reiki Master, who I am sure
has been a teacher of mine for many lifetimes.

Black Elk, 1863-1950

Black Elk, my Reiki Guide. I am honoured that my dedication to Reiki was rewarded with the energy and guidance of such a powerful and well-respected medicine man.

CHAPTER 8

Glen

I can honestly say I have never known such ease with a person as I felt on meeting Glen again after all those years, and it continued over the entire few days that we had together. We spoke about where life had taken us since we last saw each other, our failed relationships, our journeys, our battles, and our victories. We covered pretty much everything and still had more to talk about! Communication was so easy, even when we had different points of view about things. That evening, we went into Tain (my local town) and had a wonderful meal. When we got back to my house, I went and got the St Christopher I'd found a few weeks back. As Glen held it in his hands, his eyes welled up as he told me he had received it as a gift from his sister. I didn't know that, but it certainly amplified just how much Glen had held me in his heart all those years ago to have given me such a special gift. Glen's sister passed away when he was a teenager; she had battled her own demons and never recovered, which led her to take her own life. She had been like a mother to him after his parents' separation, and their bond was especially strong because they had already lost another sibling years earlier through a tragic accident. The whole family had endured so much heartache and loss, but you would never know that from Glen, who was and still is so strong and has such deep and profound understanding about life and its cycles. He innately understood that things happen in life that we cannot control, but also that we can choose how we respond and how we carry on. Glen has never chosen to feel sorry for himself, to blame, or hold hatred and sorrow in his heart. Of all the people I've known in life, here was someone nobody could judge for feeling that life had dealt him an unlucky card and perhaps even feeling sorry for himself, but he couldn't have been further away from that. Glen's outlook is very humbling.

My heart warmed even more towards him, and as we spoke of the night that I received the necklace, he sat up, pulled up his t-shirt and showed me a scar on his back, right where his sacral chakra is. He asked if I remembered how he got it, and it all started coming back to me. We were in his house, lying in bed one night; we'd been out with friends but had gone back home early. As we were chatting away, he leaned over, opened his bedside drawer, and pulled out his St Christopher and put in on me. Just then we heard the front door open. It was his dad. We could hear his footsteps coming up the stairs. Glen dived to the bottom of the bed to pull up the covers (and protect my modesty!) and as he did, he scratched his back on the bed post. It must have hurt, but he managed to cover me up just in time before his dad opened the bedroom door to ask if he had any cigarettes. It was at that moment our fates together were sealed, although we couldn't possibly have realised it at the time. The interruption by his dad meant that he never did explain who gave him the St Christopher, and so I never fully grasped the importance of it until we reunited fifteen years later. I had no idea the scar was still so prominent, nor did I understand the significance of the scar being on his sacral chakra. The sacral chakra is not only our centre of sexuality but also creation. There was no way I could ignore all these signs and abundant synchronicities as the pieces all slowly came together.

I went on to tell Glen about the male birds that had been making an appearance over the last few weeks and the strong sense I had that a male was going to enter my life. He told me that on his train journey from Aberdeen to Inverness, he too had seen a heron, and that it flew alongside the train long enough to catch his eye and for him take note of it. I was stunned again by our synchronicity — it was like a script from a film — pieces fitting so perfectly together, and suddenly another realisation hit me. I realised then that my journey back home to Fraserburgh a few months back to heal my past and situations that had caused pain and hurt was not the closing of a door to that time and place, but rather, a reopening of a door to true bliss and the kind of happiness I couldn't even imagine. Through my meditations and Reiki healing, I had done that. It was only making itself known now because of the deep-rooted work I'd done on myself, and because I had stopped closing myself off to the love the Universe had for me by focusing only on unconditional self-love. It was, and still is, a profound moment of enlightenment for me, an acknowledgment that when I align my energies with

Source, my life's path can be lit up in the most amazing ways. This is true for all of us, but only if you're willing to surrender to a path of learning to love yourself unconditionally and before anything else. I didn't know where the next part of my journey was going to lead, but I did know that it was a journey I was willing to undertake. There was a reason for all these things that were happening to bring Glen and me together; there was a reason for everything that had happened between us since we first met all those years ago.

Becoming aligned with who I really am has allowed me to view my life's events from an even broader perspective. What's more, Glen has had this same epiphany. I remember him saying once that he now saw everything and how it all fitted into place. He expressed that he felt we should have never split up when we were younger. I told him that, in fact, everything had happened exactly as it was supposed to. I understood why he would think that, but for me, it was an even bigger sign that all of the things I'd been through in life had brought me to this point. Had I not made the choices I had and gone through all the shit, I would have never chosen to devote so much time to me and my energetic alignment. Glen and I could not have appreciated each other in the way that we do now, had we not both gone through our separate journeys, only for the paths we walked to merge into one again, in the most beautiful way.

We crammed so much into our weekend together, and I can honestly say I've never kissed someone so much in all my life or smiled so much, and the happiness and elation that I felt was only the beginning. The Universe, once again, had delivered to me exactly what I needed at exactly the right time. Had I been given the option a few months earlier, I may not have chosen for it to work out as it did because at that time, I was focused on creating a new career and the life that would stem from a new working environment. I wouldn't have chosen it because, if I'm truthful, I don't think I would have trusted it. You see, we must remain open for things to manifest in the right way, for our highest and greatest good. It's in the letting go of control that we can feel what it is like to have true faith and trust in the Universal laws and energies. But the Universe doesn't deliver the things we *think* we want; it delivers the things we energetically want and need.

The morning Glen was leaving to go back to Fraserburgh was one of mixed emotions. We were both so happy, but at the same time, there was a sinking feeling in the pit of my stomach because I knew he had to leave. It didn't help that the radio was playing song after song about leaving and goodbyes. I had noticed the songs and how they were reflecting our feelings but wasn't about to say it out loud, so Glen did! We were so in sync with regards to thoughts that we were finishing each other's sentences and knowing intuitively what the other was thinking before it was said. We got to Inverness and went for some food before his train came, and I remember him holding my hands and saying, "This is going to get serious, isn't it? I mean it already is," and as I cried, I replayed Theresa's question to me just before his arrival,

"Is this Glen Morrice someone who could make you lose focus of where you're going?" "Of course not," I had said! "It's just going to be a bit of fun, nothing serious." And I'd meant it. At that time, I wasn't looking for a serious relationship. In my mind, I was so sure that it was only going to be a bit of fun between two like-minded individuals. But as I gazed into his eyes, I knew I had already signed my fate; I knew that my life from now on would be one with Glen in it. I didn't know the details, it was far too early for that, and I didn't need to know; I just knew what was in my heart, that it was real, and that this was something I couldn't walk away from, even if I tried. Our destiny was already written, and we were honouring a contract that we'd both signed up for a lifetime ago. All our searching had brought us back together, and I was not about to throw this away. I was embracing it with everything I had. The excitement in my heart overruled the sadness of him leaving, and that's how I knew it was right.

We held on to each other for as long as we possibly could before he boarded the train. The feeling of connection, as our bodies, minds and souls embraced, was incredible. I knew this was a beginning, not an ending, so I was full of anticipation about what would happen next for us. I also knew that I had nothing to do and that it would all unfold in the right way, at the right time.

Nonetheless, I cried all the way home. But the underlying emotions were ones of amazement at how the Universe can orchestrate the most beautiful scenarios for us. Because I had committed myself to developing a deeper connection and understanding of my life and the journeys it's taken me on, I could see the bigger picture. Without this insight, I could have — and probably would have — missed the opportunity that was being presented to me because it wasn't in a way that I had imagined. But through releasing the need for total control, I was allowing more of what I needed to come into my life. And I needed Glen to be part of my life.

When I got back home to the farm, and into my house, the most intense smell of Issey Miyake came at me from all directions. I wondered why Glen had gone back into the house before we left, and now I knew; he had sprayed his aftershave everywhere — on my bed, the sofa, cushions, and curtains. It was a thoughtful touch, and the scent of him lingered for days and kept the frequency and intensity of energy going. It's still one of my favourite smells, especially on Glen. Whenever I smell it, I am transported back to that magical time. Years on, my feelings for Glen are just as strong. Even after nine years, I can honestly say I don't just love him, I am 100% hook, line, and sinker in love with him. I am thankful for that feeling every day, and I appreciate more than ever that this love came into my life because I decided to love me, first and foremost. Through the desire to know and understand myself, and my thoughts and actions, I was able to open up my energy to what my true desires and purpose in life are, and then to create my life more deliberately. Self-empowerment at its best!

CHAPTER 9

～

New Bonds

The weeks that followed were a whirlwind of emotions, experiences, and adventures. While Glen was offshore, we kept in touch through email and phone calls, and when he returned home, we spent as much time together as possible. To begin with, our time together was limited because Glen had two daughters from his previous relationship — a ten year old and two year old. Relationship breakdowns are never easy on anyone, but it is especially difficult when there are children involved. I never wanted to come between Glen and his kids, so I made no demands on his time. If it was his time to have them, we arranged our visits around this, and for a little while it worked.

As time went on, news of our relationship reached his ex, and the inevitable consequences of resentment and change reared their ugly heads. Soon, Glen's visitations rights with the girls were affected, and he even had to go through heart breaking and gruelling court cases just to secure his basic rights as a father. It wasn't an easy time for anyone and the emotional toll it took was great. It's never easy when a relationship breaks down, I know this only too well from my own experiences, and although we are aware when things have gone too far to be fixed, it still takes time for our emotions to be processed and for us to adjust to the change. There was obvious pain for his two daughters as well, especially the eldest who was very much daddy's girl. The disintegration of their family unit, and then not being allowed to see her beloved dad, left a huge void in her life. Glen and I were not immune to the effects of what was going on, either. Here we were at the early stages of our life together, a time when life should have been carefree, but there was a constant cloud hanging over us. I could offer compassion and a level of understanding through a different perspective, but I had not gone through the experience of having children yet, so I couldn't relate to how he was feeling, that was not possible, and at times this left me feeling very helpless.

Once Glen was not allowed access to his children, he stopped going home to Fraserburgh during his time on shore. He was working in Canada at the time, three weeks on and three weeks off, and he had his flights changed so he flew straight into Inverness airport when he was off. It was too painful for him to be at home, and the effort he tried to make to see the girls only made things worse. Sometimes we have to put a little distance between ourselves and our problems so that the Universe has time to figure things out. There were so many components and other people involved in this, it was the best thing to do at the time. Watching him suffer through it all was difficult, especially when trying to stay in alignment and create a positive mindset.

For the few months that Glen stayed with me in the Highlands, I was able to, for the most part, put aside what was going on, as well as the hatred that his ex had towards me and our re-lationship. We enjoyed spending time with each other and going on adventures. I saw so much of the Highlands with Glen; we would set off in the car and just get lost on purpose, to see where we would end up. It was great. I recommend this to anyone, es-pecially if you tend to try and control every aspect of your life. Just let go and see where life takes you! It helped that we were in Scotland because of the scenery, the wildlife, and the energy that comes from being in the mountains and glens. Sometimes it would just be the two of us, and other times we went on ad-ventures with friends. These trips had a profound healing effect on Glen. Being in nature helps our energies realign anyhow, but our impromptu adventures were giving him freedom and time to be with his thoughts and explore various perspectives on his situation. Clarity of thought, and clarity in those moments of alignment, helped him dig deep to find a way through, rather than burying his head in the sand as he would have done before.

When we were at the farm, I started to give Glen Reiki treat-ments. By his own admission, he was a "non-believer," but as ear-ly as his very first session, he was converted. There was no doubt left in his mind. He would go into deep states of consciousness every time, which was exactly how his body and mind needed to be in order to truly heal. Every time he'd come round, he would comment on the bright colours that filled his mind's eye. For someone who had once claimed energy work was "a load of shit," his intuition and connection to the experience was off the scale.

On one occasion, when he had left to go back to Canada, he messaged me to say that he'd arrived and that they were en route to get the helicopter to the rig. The snow had started there, and it was particularly heavy, so as he was travelling, I sent him some Reiki to keep him safe and protected. Like always, when I activate my Reiki channel, I call on the presence and energy of Archangel Michael and Archangel Raphael (two of my close guides who have always worked with me). Within about ten minutes, my phone rang; it was Glen asking if I was sending him Reiki. I asked why he thought that, and his reply was, "Every time I close my eyes, all I can see is blue and green." Those happened to be the colours of Archangel Michael (blue) and Archangel Raphael (green). I love it when things like this happen, especially over a distance. He couldn't believe it, but at the same time he knew it was real, and I'm pretty sure it was at that moment that any lingering doubts he may have had with regards to energy healing melted away and left him a true believer. The Reiki helped Glen develop a new perspective on the situation he was going through with his children and ex. It was still tough, but he realised that he had to hold the situation, and everyone in it, in a place of love. This new perspective allowed the Universe the time it needed for things to resolve at the right time for everyone.

A few months later, Glen attended a court date and was awarded access to his girls again. This was great news, but it would still take a while for everyone's emotions to settle and adjust to yet another change. It had been months since Glen had been with his girls, and he was a very hands-on dad. They had to get used to each other again, within a new setting, in which they were no longer a family unit with their mum. Now, when Glen was on shore, we were travelling down to Fraserburgh again. If I had work commitments, then he would go down alone, but if not, I joined him; he wanted me there for moral support, and the kids weren't sleeping overnight with us yet. As much as I wanted to begin the process of getting to know them, it was still too soon, so I kept my distance. On the days that Glen had the girls, I stayed away from the house, or he'd take them out for the day. I was so happy for them. The youngest was only two, so she was unaware of what was going on, but his elder daughter was very aware and very close to her dad. It had been hard on her missing her dad so much, and he certainly missed her too. This time of re-bonding was crucial for them all, so I did the only thing I knew to help, and that was to give them the space they needed and to see and hold them all in the space of pure love and light, for the highest and greatest good.

The process of integrating our relationship with Glen's daughters took some time, and like all extended families, we had our occasional ups and downs. It takes time to deal with our emotions and process them; our minds aren't always able to keep up with things that are happening in our external world. Even for someone like me, who had been studying myself for several years, it was a somewhat difficult adjustment. However, I was able to see the bigger picture of what was going on, and I was confident in the knowledge that time would be the greatest healer and that I had to keep my thoughts and feelings positive. Most importantly, I had to be patient.

Patience had never been my strong suit, but I was getting better at it. I knew that if I wanted the best outcome for everyone, I had to remain gracious and see this situation for what it was — my next life lesson. We have no control over the free will of others, which means we cannot force our views or beliefs onto anyone, and we cannot be fooled into thinking that our way is always the right way. What is right for us doesn't equate to what is right for everyone. We all have lessons to learn through the experiences in our lives, and we must never presume to know what other people's lessons are. It's simply none of our business, just as the opinions of others are none of our business. Through learning this truth, we enable ourselves to develop control over our own emotions and stop being reactive to what life throws at us. If every time during this process I had let the views or words of others dictate my feelings, I would not be writing this book, nor living the life I am now. And I most certainly would not be content with who and what I am. It is more likely that I would still be blaming others for my shortcomings, playing the victim in life, and going round in the same circles that I'd wasted so much time in before. This was not an option, obviously. I couldn't and wouldn't ever go back to being that empty, lost shell I had once been. There was purpose to my life, and this path was beginning to shine a light on what that purpose was. I would never go back.

I spent a lot of time meditating and visualising everyone involved in the highest possible light. I spent time generating feelings of pure joy and happiness within me first and then projecting those emotions into the visualisations I had of them. I didn't get too specific with the scenes I created in my mind; I just saw and held the image of everyone that was part of this situation as happy, laughing, loving, communicating, and being supportive of each other, for the highest and greatest good. The shift didn't happen overnight; sometimes, it felt like giant leaps were taken, and other times, it felt like we would go backwards. But that is the natural state of change. Sometimes, the physical factors take time to catch up to the vibrational change that is underway. We never actually go back because that's impossible. Even when we feel like we're not making any headway, we are still moving forward, and that is the main thing to keep at the forefront of your mind when you find yourself going through tricky life changes such as these. As long as you are holding the feelings that match the thoughts of your intentions, you will always be progressing. And forward movement is forward movement, no matter how slow it may feel at the time. If everything happened instantly, we'd spend a hell of a lot of time trying to undo things! It's important to understand and accept the natural flow and timing of things, and the easiest way to get into this flow is to be in the present moment as much as possible, which takes practise, but reaps priceless rewards. Whenever you catch your train of thought being anywhere else other than in the present, stop and pull it back into the now.

Glen's time at home was split between the farm with me and Fraserburgh when he had the girls, which meant my time with him was also split. Our relationship was strong, and we had both committed to each other and wanted to grow our relationship and see where it would take us. It was coming up to a year since we had got together, and we both knew that we couldn't continue to commute the three hours between Tain and Fraserburgh in the long term. A decision would have to be made regarding where we would live permanently. Never in my wildest dreams did I expect I would return to Fraserburgh — it was a notion I hadn't needed to entertain — but I found myself in a situation where it became an option I had to consider. However, I was a different person to the eighteen-year-old heroin addict I had been when I left that place, alone, scared, and confused. I was no longer the awkward, self-deprecating girl I once believed I was, and who I believed others saw me to be. I had alienated most of my friends through my addiction and the relationship with my manipulative and controlling boyfriend. That is who I was when I left, so naturally, I thought that was how people would remember me if I were to go back. I wasn't preoccupied with people's views of me, but I'd only ever gone back for a weekend here and there to see old friends, and that time I went back to send Reiki, so this train of thought was new to me. It was a chapter in my life I thought I'd turned the page on.

It was very clear to me that this needed to happen, although the thought of it wasn't filling me with excited anticipation.

Initially, I felt worry, panic, and anxiety, but I could also see how I'd been inadvertently preparing for this moment for some time. Glen and I weren't only destined to be together in this lifetime, we were destined to start afresh, together in our home town; it would almost be like picking up where we left off, but fifteen years later and with a lot more experience under our belts. At first, he was filled with guilt when we spoke about it. He knew how I felt about Fraserburgh and the person I was when I left there, so he was worried about how going back and seeing the old faces and places that held those dark memories would affect me. There was a time when I'd become physically sick whenever I thought about that period of my life and be transported back to the negativity I associated with it. So actually being back there, walking through the streets again, and seeing the same faces would be far more intense than just reminiscing about it. Honestly, I didn't know how I would cope with it. I worried that it might reactivate the vibration that I'd worked so hard at removing until anxiety and fear took hold of me. I also knew that Glen wanted me there but didn't want to ask it of me. I could understand his point of view, but his feelings of guilt were nothing to what I would feel knowing I was the reason he couldn't be close to his children. This was something I just couldn't and wouldn't allow, so I made the decision that if we were to stay together and take our relationship to the next level — which we both definitely wanted — I would have to be the one to up sticks, move back to Fraserburgh, and face my fears head on.

And so, the decision was made. I would leave the sanctuary of my Highland home, my friends, my business — everything — to go back to Fraserburgh with my love. Was I scared? Yes! Was I sure it was the right thing to do? Absolutely. The love which was gifted to me from the Universe in the form of Glen was something that I had received because I chose to take the time and develop my relationship with myself first. I had returned to my Source within and taken responsibility for all my choices. I'd stopped playing the victim. I had found the true eternal love that is always within us when we choose to align with it, and that was epic. The power of this, the energy that came from the two of us being united again in the way that we were, made me realise it was my destiny to go back to Fraserburgh. The Universe had been giving me signs, and through the piecing together of these, I had confidence and faith in the path I was following. That was enough to override any fears that my ego was trying to hold me back with.

CHAPTER 10

Back to the Start

What a whirlwind the last year had been; it was still hard to believe everything that had happened and how it had all worked out. From the first appearance of the male pheasant and the heron, to finding the St Christopher pendant, to the magical return of Glen into my life. I felt truly blessed to be so loved by him. I'd always felt that unconditional love was possible, but until you actually experience it, it can seem like a pipe dream. I am here to tell it you that it's not. It does exist, it is there for everyone to find, but first, we must be willing to do the work on ourselves and strip back all the layers of crap that have built up on us over the years. It's a small price to pay for the joy you receive from becoming re-aligned with your true state of being.

The move back went very smoothly, which was another reassuring sign that I was doing the right thing. I started to pack up my life into boxes, and every time we went back down to Fraserburgh, a carload would go with me, until all that was left was some clothes and miscellaneous items I wasn't taking with me. I finished up with all my clients, and the support and well wishes I received were truly humbling. I realised I had really made strong connections with all of my clients, and I was so grateful to and for them. Setting up this business had been a leap of faith, and their belief in me and my abilities helped me keep going in the early days, which, in turn, helped me have faith in myself and my ability to achieve whatever I set my mind to, further adding to my confidence and self-reliance. Saying goodbye to them was hard, but they were all so happy for me.

It was a beautiful weekend when we left the Highlands. I had one final work booking to complete at the Torridon, before I left the North. The weather was perfect, and the wedding I was there for couldn't have gone any better. Having Glen there with me was the icing on the cake. As I worked, he hung out with Robert's husband Bruce and their doggies, and at night we enjoyed good food, fine wine, and the company of two very dear friends. It was a chance for me to say goodbye to Torridon, as well, because once I moved back to Fraserburgh, a three-and-a-half-hour commute for work would be out of the question. Robert and I had first visited the Torridon when we worked together at Skibo Castle, and now, years later, he was managing the hotel, and I was leaving. It was the end of an era, that's for sure. I'm so glad I spent my last weekend there with very dear friends. It was the perfect farewell. I knew the next goodbye would be the toughest, and I wasn't looking forward to it at all.

Now all that was left for me to do before starting a new chapter was to return to the farm for the very last time, pick up Louis, and say goodbye to my best friend in the world, my partner in crime, Theresa. There is not enough time or words for me to convey just how much she means to me. It's the type of friendship that will withstand anything, but even that was no comfort in knowing that she wouldn't just be ten minutes away over the Dornoch bridge. This parting was going to leave a hole. We had been each other's crutch and shoulder to cry on for so long. We understood each other's craziness, could read each other, and we always knew instinctively what the other needed. I think what made it worse was that Theresa was just coming out of a dark period in her own life. She was on her way out of it, but by leaving I felt like I was throwing her back into the deep end just as she was nearing the shore. My only comfort was that I knew she had Xavier in her life now, and I knew he would help her move on.

Theresa and Xavier had been looking after the farm and Louis while we were in Torridon. Everything was packed; I just had to get Louis in the car and say my goodbyes. I knew it wasn't goodbye, Theresa would always be my best friend, but we wouldn't be together anymore, not like we had been up until that point. I reminded myself that change is inevitable and often for the good. And with my newfound understanding and alignment, this change would not leave me emotionally devastated like it would have done a few years earlier. Despite this, it hurt like hell, and I started crying immediately when I hugged her. It was silly really, we were going on holiday to Malaga in a few weeks' time, but this goodbye was marking a major shift, the turning of a page into a new, unread chapter. It really was a bittersweet moment.

With the car packed, I handed my keys back and said good-bye to my Highland sanctuary for the very last time. As we left, I realised another significant factor about the timing of it all; it was the beginning of April — the start of spring. I was following the energies of nature, aligned perfectly with new beginnings, new growth, and fresh starts. This awareness filled me with joy, and I drew further comfort from it that the changes I was undertaking were being supported by the energies of my world. I was flowing down with the river, not against it. I could simply let go and trust that where I was heading and what would unfold along the way was all meant to be — it was all part of the bigger plan for my highest and greatest good — and as long as I stayed aligned with my Source and my true state of being, I couldn't go wrong.

The journey down the road to Fraserburgh was wonderful. We were like two love-struck teenagers absorbed in each other's energies, being carried along by the excitement of what lay before us. We made a pit stop at my parents' house which was only an hour from Fraserburgh. It was a welcome breather and a chance for Louis to get out of the car and stretch his legs. He had been meowing loudly to ensure we knew that he wasn't happy! It was refreshing to think that the drive from my parents' house to Fraserburgh would be the only distance I would have to cover when I wanted to visit them from then on. When I was young and living in Fraserburgh with my family, we would make the journey up to Keith every weekend that my dad was home. He was from Keith originally, and up until I was twenty one, my paternal granny was there too, along with most of his thirteen brothers and sisters. And now it was me who would be based in Fraserburgh, travelling up to Keith to visit them. There was such a beautiful synchronicity in the patterns in life coming round full circle. I liked this notion very much, and it spoke to my heart and gave me yet more comfort. I was so happy to be closer to them again.

With the last leg of the journey over, we arrived in Fraserburgh, and all that was left to do was for me to get the last of my stuff out of the car and into the house. At least the unpacking wouldn't be stressful; most of my stuff was already there, now it was just a case of making it feel like home, and that would all fall into place in its own time. I had done it! I had made a life-changing decision and followed through with it, but I didn't know what was coming next. I had no work to focus on, no real structure or even routine to follow because it was all new. Although I'd been travelling down for weekends before I made the move permanent, when I went back up to the farm, I had a structure in place that I could fall back into. Now I had to create a new one. I was not giving it too much attention, but I knew I was going to feel it when Glen went away off shore. I'd be on my own, I wouldn't have the security blanket of him being there with me, and this did cause a certain amount of anxiety. But for now, I knew it would serve me no good to start down that train of thought, so I remained blissful in the moment I was in, happy that I was in love with a wonderful man who was in love with me, happy to be blessed with something that most people spend their whole life looking for but never find.

Any fears I had about settling in were soon set aside as I did the one thing I knew I could, so when they did creep in, I stopped the thought in their tracks before they could take hold. It didn't take long for the faces of old to make an appearance, but I'm glad to say it was all good ones. I wasn't merely concerned about seeing unwelcome faces from my past; Glen had been with his ex for ten years before they split, and we all shared some mutual friends who I had grown up with too. Would I be accepted back? What would their memories of me be? I even talked different now and the local dialect, which was once my native tongue, had not passed over my lips for many years. I'd had to lose it because no one up north knew what I was saying, let alone the many American and English clients I had. It made me feel somewhat self-conscious knowing I had changed so much, and none of these old friends had witnessed any of it. Some weren't fazed by it, some thought it was great, and others, I could tell, were taken aback by it. But I needed to remind myself that it wasn't important what others thought, and I certainly was under no obligation to offer justification for anything. If I did come across anyone who was acting weird towards me, then that would be because that was the vibration I was offering. What really mattered, in this case, was for me to remember all the work I had put into myself, into aligning my energies, living my truth, and connecting with the Source energy that was part of me.

The insecurities which were coming to the surface weren't new; actually, I'd dealt with them before, but only in the capacity I was able to handle at the time. Now that I was back, another layer of the onion had been peeled away, ready for me to heal at a deeper level than I'd been able to before. When wounds and paradigms run deep, sometimes we have to re-visit them a few times for their removal to be fully effective, so when you view it through this perspective, it makes sense that it takes time, effort, and patience for them to be completely eradicated and before new, healthy, positive thoughts can take their place. This awareness was a saviour. It allowed me comfort through the understanding of why I had to go through this lesson again, without which it would have been so easy for frustration and resentment to set in, thereby causing resistance and sabotaging my growth.

Over the next couple of weeks, I eased myself back into Fraserburgh, into my new home, and some sort of new routine. I started to unpack my crystals and place them around the house. It was so nice to see my beautiful, energetic babies out of their wrapping and doing what they do best by helping to shape the flow of energy and create a harmonious atmosphere. Meditating wasn't coming easily to me, there seemed to be a constant distraction whenever I tried, and it felt like I was learning to train my brain all over again. I will admit I did find this very frustrating, which I knew was only adding resistance to the situation, but I did my best not to force anything. So there were a lot of walks in nature, soaking up the stillness that life had to offer in other ways (there are always alternatives on offer, we just have to change our perception so that the solution has an opportunity to present itself to us), and it was nice to be sharing these moments with Glen before it was time for him to go off shore again. The countryside is so different around Fraserburgh compared with up in the Highlands. One place I had missed was the beautiful beach. The ruggedness of the coastline in the northeast corner of Scotland is breath-taking, and the history associated with it is fascinating. Reconnecting with my home was actually turning out to be full of enjoyable surprises, and Glen and I always love an adventure!

Glen was leaving for work shortly, but luckily, I had only a week to fill between his departure and flying off to Malaga for a girly holiday with Theresa and another mutual friend. So, before Glen went away, we bought some paint and a few other items we needed. I was going to inject some freshness into the house, create a new ambience — a new sanctuary — and I was excited to get my inner decorator loose. I've always enjoyed home decorating. I see our homes as an extension of our creative energy. We spend so much time in them, so they need to compliment us, stimulate us, and soothe us all in the right amounts. When our homes work right for us, the flow of energy can flow well, and we can be at our most productive instead of stagnant, or worse still, full of non-productive habits that create more negative conditioning in our behaviour. Never underestimate the power that your surroundings have over your wellbeing; if they are not in alignment with you, you will feel it.

When Glen left, I got busy with a paintbrush and got used to my own company again, creating a space that felt like home, and building myself up from the inside out by managing my energy properly. The meditation was getting easier, but I was far from the astral projection and out-of-body experiences I had been having before. I knew it would return when I was ready for it, so I turned to more self-Reiki for the time, which was just what I needed. There's always healing to do on ourselves. Nothing stays the same for any length of time, everything is in constant motion, and we need to apply this awareness to ourselves, especially during times of transition, or we risk becoming overwhelmed, anxious, fearful and, ultimately, alter our point of attraction. And that is when the train of negative momentum begins to go full steam ahead. But I knew better, and I was not about to let that happen. By the time I left for Malaga, most of the house was transformed. I had created a space that felt like home, and it was a beautiful balance for both of our energies. Louis was settling in, and he was making lots of cat friends and enjoying becoming top cat in a new neighbourhood. Life was good, and I was off on my holidays. I had so much to feel thankful for. I was happy.

CHAPTER 11

~

Trouble in Paradise

Malaga was great from start to finish. We lay in the sun all day, only stopping to eat, drink, and go on gentle walks. At night, we'd get dressed up and go out and sample all of the fantastic cuisine that there was on offer — there was a particular seafood restaurant that was just amazing. I've always enjoyed the way of life in the Mediterranean; they have such an easy, laid-back attitude, it's impossible for it not to rub off on you, it's somewhere I could see myself living at some point in life.

Glen was working out of a shipyard in Singapore and staying in a hotel at nights. Now this is nothing new, and when work is like that for him, it means more drinking with the boys in the evening. That in itself isn't a problem, other than the fact that Glen cannot hold his drink because he isn't a heavy drinker. Funnily enough, while I was in Malaga, I received more drunken phone calls from him than he did from me, and considering I was the one on holiday and he was the one at work, it was beginning to grate on me a bit. I appreciated and understood that in his line of work there are times that you have to go along with it, but there are also times when you can make your own decisions and not just act like one of the boys. And this type of behaviour was uncharacteristic for Glen.

After a particularly bad drunken phone call, I chose to address this issue with Glen because I knew that if the shoe were on the other foot, he wouldn't be too happy about it either. He apologised and said he could see where I was coming from. He understood that it wasn't that I expected him to not go out with the boys, but I didn't expect to have to listen to him puking over the phone every night and talking crap after a night on the booze. It was not at all what I'd signed up for in a relationship. I wanted someone who was his own man, not someone who caved in to peer pressure from the boys every night.

He promised that he wouldn't go out the following evening. Instead, he'd meet everyone for food and a couple of beers and then head back to the hotel. He was, after all, starting work at 5 am. But it didn't turn out that way, and I called him out on it — again. And again, he apologised. I could sense that he was genuine, but he also didn't want the boys thinking he was "under the thumb," or being told what to do by his woman! We said goodbye, and he went back in to meet up with the lads. I was about to head out, so I went back into our villa when my phone rang. It was Glen. I picked up and realised pretty quickly that he'd pocket dialled me, and what I heard send shock waves through me and made me question everything that I thought was true and real about us. I could hear his mates taunting him, asking if I was giving him grief, but it was Glen's response — the attitude that I could hear in the words as he spoke them — that I was not prepared for. Trying to act the tough guy, his response was: *"If that's how she's going to be, she can fucking pack her bags and get out. I'm not putting up with that shit!"* It felt like my world was collapsing. Hearing Glen talk that way, saying those horrible words, was devastating, and I began to shake uncontrollably. I felt physically sick. I had been so sure of him, so sure of how we had been brought back together, so sure of my guidance and intuition. How could I have got it so wrong? I had left the home I loved to move back to Fraserburgh and make a new home and life with him. I did that so that he would never have to face the option of moving away from his girls. Had my sacrifices all been for nothing? A million thoughts were racing through my mind. A million different conversations. They were, of course, all one-sided but they created all the raw emotions that felt so real, and if I allowed them to continue, I would be shifting my point of attraction and manifesting all sorts of situations and things that I didn't want. I stopped to take a few deep breaths, to try and slow my heart that was still beating out of my chest, to slow my thoughts that were by now spinning out of control, and as I did, I knew that at this moment I was reacting to what had happened. I was allowing this event to take over. There was only one thing I needed to focus on, and that was regaining my power. I needed to stop reacting and start responding.

I hung the phone up and collected myself. My head was still all over the place, but I knew that I was of no service to myself like this. I needed to calm down. With long, slow, deep breaths I focused on grounding my energies. I did this until my body stopped shaking and I could feel my breathing return to a normal rate. By this point, Theresa and Michelle knew that something was up, so I went outside and told them. Theresa got it straight away; she knew Glen, she knew me, and she was able to see past it. But at the same time, she also knew what I had been through in my previous relationship, how I'd picked myself up and vowed never to be manipulated or treated in a way that I knew I was not deserving of, so she understood my rage and disappointment in Glen's hurtful words, all to be one of the boys!

About twenty minutes had passed since I'd overheard Glen's awful speech, and I felt ready to call him back. He answered and I could still hear the attitude in his voice, so I knew he was still standing in the bar surrounded by his workmates. Very calmly I told him that he'd pocket dialled me and that I had heard every-thing he said to his mates. There was complete silence on his end of the line. I didn't give him a chance to respond; I simply told him that he wasn't big nor clever, and that he would never have the opportunity to disrespect me like that ever again, and then I hung up the phone. He panicked straight away, and my phone started to ring on repeat. I didn't answer, so he left multiple voice messages. He was distraught, and he knew he'd seriously messed up. I'd never heard such anxiety and fear in his voice, ever, and I even felt sorry for him. The thing is, I knew he didn't really mean it, but I couldn't betray myself, my values, and my self-worth. I poured a glass a wine and drank it in the sunshine, partly to make him sweat a bit more, partly to remind myself that I didn't need anyone to feel complete, and to remind myself that if I was going to have someone in my life, it was because I wanted them in it, NOT because I needed them.

When I did eventually call him back, my heart started beating uncontrollably again. I loved Glen as I had never loved or thought I could love someone, and that's why I felt so betrayed by his remarks. He answered instantly and he wasn't in the bar anymore. He was back in his hotel room, feeling sorry for himself, feeling stupid, sick, and worried. When he heard me saying that I'd overheard everything, the realisation of what he'd done sank in. One of the workmates had told him not to worry about it, to which he responded by saying, "After all she's done for me, how could I say those things when I don't even mean them? She's the one thing in my life that is real, and now I've lost her."

I didn't want to add salt to his wounds, there was no need for that, but I did want him to realise the impact his actions had had on me. He admitted that he was just trying to be "one of the boys," and as much as I could understand this, I pointed out that the opinions of these people, some of whom he would never see again, had mattered more to him in that moment and that he'd reacted instead of responding with his truth, just to fit in with them — a bunch of testosterone-driven assholes. One of the reasons I fell for Glen was precisely that he didn't have that need to be one of the boys, so for him to act like this towards me was not who he was. In fact, it was completely out of alignment with his higher self. He kept asking what I was going to do. Would I be there when he got home? And the truth was, I didn't know, and I wasn't going to let my thoughts run wild at that point. I was going to enjoy the remainder of my holiday.

The girls and I were hitting the town that night. Michelle had managed to keep Theresa and me away from the nightlife all week, but not this night, and it couldn't have come at a better time. I reassured Glen that I wouldn't be doing anything for him to be worried about but also reminded him that after his actions, he'd lost the right to hold any expectations over how I was going to conduct myself that evening. I was going out to have fun, and that's exactly what we did. I'm laughing on the inside as I write this because I can remember hearing Michelle shouting, "It's five o'clock in the morning" at Theresa and me as we walked barefoot along the promenade after coming out of a bar. My response was, "So fucking what?" We got in a taxi, headed back to our apartment, and slept off the alcohol that we'd consumed. It was a good night; we laughed, we danced, and we enjoyed every moment. It was just what I needed after the bombshell that Glen had dropped on me.

When my eyes peeled themselves open the next day, I knew he'd be waiting for me to get in touch. There were a couple of messages on my phone, and I knew he would have been desperate for me to make contact, probably in a state of panic and worry. I can only imagine how unbearable the wait must have been.

I don't even think I heard the phone ring on my end he was so quick to answer. The first thing he did was ask if I would fly to Singapore as soon as I got home. He had bought the flights and arranged everything. All I had to do was agree. It would be another four weeks before he was due to fly home, and he was aware how much hurt and betrayal I felt because of his actions, so the only thing that mattered to him (and me) now was fixing it. If I was going to move forward with this new life that was being created with him, I needed to know that this was never going to happen again. I really didn't care about him going out with the boys, but I needed to know that no matter where he was, or who he was with, he had my back and respected me. I now valued me more than anything, and things had to feel absolutely right, so I agreed to go.

I flew out to Singapore just two days after returning home from Malaga. The start of us living together was already proving to be full of surprises — not ones I had expected — but then, the Universe does work in mysterious ways to deliver us our deepest desires.

CHAPTER 12

~

Sweet Singapore

It was a long haul getting to Singapore from Fraserburgh, even with the most direct flights. I had never travelled such a long distance before, so I was more than a little bit nervous but also full of excitement. Every single step of the way, the Universe was giving me little signs, and the right people turned up to help with any queries I had before I even had to look for them. My experience of travelling was smooth, no delays, and no dramas or obstacles appearing in my path. I even ended up sitting next to a man who was going out to work on the same drillship Glen was on. All these signs were telling me I was in the right place, even though that came about through an experience I would never have chosen.

I arrived in Singapore roughly 24 hours after leaving my house. Glen had organised transport for me from the airport to the hotel. It was late afternoon when I arrived. I walked into the room, closed the curtains, and went straight to bed. I'm not the best at sleeping on planes, so I had a lot of sleep to catch up on.

Never have I woken up to such a warm, loving embrace. I'm not sure how long Glen had been lying next to me stroking my face. I was still so tired when I opened my eyes, there were three of him, and I could barely lift my head.

"I thought you might not come. I thought I'd lost you forever. I thought you might just get back from Malaga and pack your bags and leave." Those were the first words he spoke. I hugged him back, sat up and rubbed my eyes, and waited to wake up properly before responding. I had so many words inside me that wanted to come out, but I didn't even know where to begin. I already knew in my heart that things were going to be alright between us, but before taking that for granted, I needed there to be clear communication and understanding. I couldn't get the words out. "Say something" he begged! "I'm not going anywhere," I finally stated. "If I were, I wouldn't have come out here to be with you, but if this happens ever again, I won't even give you warning, I'll be off, and that is a promise. There are only two things I want from you: one is that you never lie to me about anything. If there are lies, there's no trust, and there's no point if there's no trust. And two, you respect me always, whether I'm there or not because *I* respect *you*." And that was it, that was all that needed to be said. I'm not one to hold a grudge, and I don't like keeping old energy active in my present. There's no way for forward movement if we stay stuck in an old vibration. I had learned time and time again over the years, the only person it hurts is yourself. There was awkwardness from Glen for a little while, which I did reassure him there was no need for, but I guess this way of doing things was new to him, and this was something that he would have to get used to.

After a coffee and a shower, we went out for my first night in Singapore. We walked through the city, had dinner, and walked some more. There was so much to take in. The city was amazing, the architecture is tremendous with such a mix of eccentric beauty from the old-style buildings to the new modern vibe. You could taste and smell the excitement of this city in the air. There is a constant buzz about the place, the food is amazing — whether you want street food or restaurant quality — and the people were very friendly, warm, and inviting. I was going to enjoy my time here, I could tell. Even though my days would be spent on my own while Glen was working, it was nice to be somewhere that I could just go out and explore without any expectations, so I couldn't be let down by anything. I was going to allow myself to be guided from moment to moment and take it all in.

I could probably write a book about the time I spent in Singapore. I truly loved it. I had so much time for reflection and to tune in to where my energy was, and I found the perfect place to do that: The Buddha Tooth Relic Temple. I can't remember the last time I was in such awe; everything about it was breathtaking. The building, the art, the sculptures, the people, but most of all, the atmosphere — I've never experienced anything like it. When you stood in the actual room that you can view the relic from, you could feel the energy in the air. It felt like electricity. It left you feeling heady like you were floating up out of your body. I've experienced this before in meditation but never as I've been awake walking around. It was very emotional, but in the most uplifting way. It was the feeling of pure love saturating your very soul. Writing this now transports me back to being there, an experience I will be forever grateful for. I visited the temple every day while I was there, and I got to take Glen there, too. He also felt the intense energies of that room, and I know it left a lasting impression on him. He commented on how that room felt. I guess when you feel energy in this way, it's hard not to acknowledge it.

My stay in Singapore was cut short after nine days because Glen had to go onto the drillship that he was working on and out of the hotel. I could have stayed, but the time was right to go. I'd got what I needed from this trip, and Glen and I were in a good place. I wouldn't have chosen for him to act in the way that he had, but it brought us together and helped him realise that a relationship with me was like nothing he'd experienced before. With open communication, we worked through what could have been a very messy situation, especially if I had let myself become reactive to his actions. Through following my heart, and not falling into old patterns of settling for less than I felt I deserved, no matter how uncomfortable it felt to be assertive and confrontational, I now had peace of mind and in my soul because I was true to me, and that felt great.

When I got back home, it felt like I was starting over on a blank slate. The first few weeks of living back in Fraserburgh had no real structure, and I had no real plan of where life was going to take me because I hadn't given it too much thought. I had made it through the house move, and then I had the holiday to distract me from creating any new focus, and then Singapore happened. It was good. I was learning to go from one moment to the next without too much thought of trajectory. But now I was back, and there was nothing for me to focus on for the first time in a long time. I needed to get my creative juices flowing again. I was missing work, missing my clients, and missing the independence that I had created for myself over the last three years. So, I started doing treatments again. I still had all my equipment and products, but it didn't take long for me to feel dissatisfaction with it. I had felt that before I left the Highlands and knew I wanted to concentrate on the holistic services I offered. I had discovered so much about the patterns and circles we go round in and how to break the negative patterns that don't serve us. I wanted to share this with people. I wanted people to feel the empowerment that I did and to be able to identify what isn't right for them. I also wanted to help people realise that they are their own magic wand, that if they needed a knight in shining armour, all they had to do was look at themselves. Yes, a seed was being planted, but it would be a while yet before I would start giving this the attention it needed. I still had some specific lessons to learn that would see some more layers of my proverbial onion peel away. There were conditioning patterns that would need to be broken down — patterns I was unaware were part of my make up — and would make themselves known in time.

Over the next few years, I settled into my life with Glen and took on the role of step mum to Glen's girls, which is a strange one when you haven't yet had children of your own. I had been around children, I loved them, and very much wanted to have my own one day, but I was used to living life for me alone, so it was a bit of a shock to the system having to adapt and change my routines for them. Also, because Glen worked away, organising time for doing things could be challenging too. Sometimes it felt like I was pushing my needs to the side, so I could accommodate everyone else. They weren't my kids. They were being raised by someone else, someone who had their own set of morals and ideals, their own ways of doing things that weren't necessarily my way of doing things, and I had to find a way in which to find the middle ground in order to give them my best while still being true to myself and honouring my needs. That was really hard. What made it more difficult was I didn't know anyone who was or had been in a similar situation to speak with about it, so there were times when I felt isolated. I was used to being in full control of what was going on in my life because most things were there of my making or wanting. Yet, here was a whole situation that involved the free will of others that I had very little control over, and how to go about handling it was all new to me. For a long time, I hadn't had to put up with negativity in my life because I wouldn't put up with it, but now it wasn't just about me, and walking away from people, or excluding them from my life, wasn't always an option. The way through this was with new perspectives, greater understanding, and learning to let go of the opinions of others, no matter how nasty and hurtful they were at times.

Life had a whole new flow to it, and I had to learn how to keep my head up in this new reality. It was hard sometimes because I didn't have the routine and structure that I'd had on the farm, plus there were a whole load of other components that had to be factored in. Everything in my life had changed, and I was starting to notice that how I felt, energetically, was also changing. I had always had a strong visual connection with energy, bright colours, and vivid images. Visualisations were as real in my mind's eye as if I were watching something on a screen. Now, things were starting to take on more feeling. I could still visualise very well, but when I was performing Reiki, the pictures that once played across the screen of my mind were coming through differently. Feelings would stir up inside me and then create an image of "knowing". It's hard to put into words, and I wasn't prepared for such a change. I suppose I just presumed that how I once saw and felt things would remain always the same. There was a niggle of doubt creeping into my mind that was causing me to think I might be losing my spiritual connection. But of course, this is ridiculous. Spirituality is not something that you lose — it's always there. After all, we are spiritual beings having a human experience, not the other way around.

On a visit up north to see Theresa, I was delighted that Norma had some free time, so I went over to see her. As soon as I started driving along the single-track roads that led to her place,

I felt everything become light within me again. This road always had an other-worldly effect on me, but it had been so long since I'd been there, and it was very refreshing. All the worries I'd created through overthinking were soon set aside once I revealed them aloud to her. I took great comfort when she told me that the same thing had happened to her, and that as time went on, her visual connection while performing Reiki also changed more to feeling or sensing energy through her intuition, which is known as *clairsentience*. She reminded me that I was going through a huge change, and although it was one I had invited, I still had to allow the energies on every level to catch up to where my head was. It's important to get out of your head from time to time; we can get too caught up with our thought patterns and inadvertently create more resistance, which we then push against, ultimately causing a perpetual game of internal tug-of-war. It's better to step out of your own way and let that shit go.

My new plan of action was to get back into the flow, and because I was in unchartered territory without the security or structure I'd been used to, I decided that as long as I ticked the boxes I needed each day for me, I could let go of the need to have a strict routine. I'd been trying to force a routine, probably because it made me feel safe, but the only thing that I was creating was more frustration at not having one, counteracting my thinking, and becoming less productive and happy in the process. I knew this was not the way, and in order for a new way to become apparent to me, I had to let it flow through me in an organic manner; the creation of my life's new structure needed to be borne of love, so that it could serve me in the right way and I could serve myself in the right way. So I decided to love the fact that my life allowed for spontaneity, and by choosing to flow with this perspective, I released my inner need to control, and with it, another layer of my onion that had been borne of fear all those years ago during my drug addiction. I can't help but muse at the irony of not being able to release this until I was back in the very place that created so much of what needed to be released. We are always exactly where we need to be in any given moment. Let the truth of this statement provide you with comfort in your moments of uncertainty.

So, flow I did, from day to day, moment to moment. Some days it was easier than others, but that's life. Contrast exists so that we can be better creators and fine-tune our desires and our experiences. And through this way of easy flow, the next step was made abundantly clear for me, for Glen, and us as a family. Our next manifestation, a creation of purpose, would be the greatest creation of all — life.

CHAPTER 13

~

Creating Life

Becoming a mother is always something that I expected to do in life, but I had always promised myself that unless I was with someone that I felt was worthy of fathering my children, then I would rather not have any. It's a huge responsibility, not just for obvious reasons, but I think that when you choose to bring another life into this world then you need to be ready to become selfless. The relationship I'd been in prior to Glen was a perfect example. He was not in a mindset that would allow him to become selfless because he hadn't yet developed the ability to take responsibility for his own actions, so I knew he didn't have the strength of character required to be the strong, providing father figure that I wanted for my children. When I was able to be honest with myself about that, it helped shine a very bright light on to the fact that our relationship was on a road to nowhere.

Glen, on the other hand, was a doer — a go-getter — and he had already proven to me what a good father he was, and that he was prepared to do anything he had to so that he could provide for his children. No matter what might happen in the future, I knew that he had good morals when it came to what kind of parent he would be, and his ability (mentally, emotionally, and physically) to provide and be a good role model.

It was approximately six months from deciding we would try for a baby to discovering that I was pregnant. I did have all the "best days" for becoming pregnant figured out, I had always been quite in tune with my cycle, but because Glen worked away for half the year, our chances of conceiving were literally halved. When I focused on this, I was creating resistance because I fixated on trying to control the how and the when, but when I removed the restrictions of this focus — BOOM — it happened.

I remember the day we found out very clearly. It was a weekend, Brooklynn and Shauna were staying, and we were going to have a late breakfast. I was a few days late, and Glen was urging me to do a test. I thought that we had missed the window of opportunity because of the dates that Glen had come home, but I agreed to go and get a test. I was only a couple of days late, and although I had noticed some changes in my body and in how I felt, I presumed that this test was going to show up negative.

As I came out of the bathroom, I could see Glen at the other end of the kitchen, Brooklynn and Shauna were at the table waiting for the food to be served up. No words said, I gazed into Glen's eyes and smiled, and he knew straight away. He came over and kissed me, and we both beamed from ear to ear. It's one of the most incredible feelings I've ever experienced. I even knew the exact day that it had happened, and it gave me so much pleasure knowing that this life had been created out of love. I had an idea in my head of how I wanted this manifestation to happen, and it was unfolding in ways that were in keeping with the intent I had.

We had a few magical weeks where the secret was just ours, and that felt magical. The smiles shared between us, the protective touches from Glen when we were out and about, created a bubble around us that was beautiful to be in. That feeling of knowing that life was growing inside me, a life that Glen and I had planned on creating, a life that would be borne of love, into a loving home, was indescribable. I felt so blessed to have found someone who I deemed special enough to share this experience with. From very early on, I knew I wanted a boy, and I knew Glen did too. There were already two girls so a boy would be nice, but there was something about the relationship between a mother and a son that I wanted, so it was decided that it was a boy, and we were so sure of this that we never even discussed names for girls.

The first few months were quite tough (but not as tough as others have it) because I had constant feelings of nausea. I never actually threw up, but the nausea was quite draining. Other than that, and the final, typically uncomfortable final month, my pregnancy was fairly plain sailing as far as pregnancies go. I held only the visions that I wanted, and apart from wanting a boy, there was one in particular that I really wanted to manifest. I read an article on veiled births, which I'd never even heard of before. But as I read the words, especially the folklore that went with it, it warmed my heart and spoke to my soul (for fisherman it means you'll never drown and in native American culture, these children would grow up to be Shamans, because they have the ability to see between the physical and spiritual realms). A veiled birth is when a child is born in their amniotic sac, and I knew that was how I wanted my son to come into the world. I think I briefly mentioned it to Glen once, but other than that, I kept it to myself and let it go, to the point where I more or less forgot about it. I also wanted a water birth. I don't know why, but it just really appealed to me, so I decided this was how it would happen. It didn't even come into my head that someone else would be in the birthing pool, or there would be any complication that would prevent me from having this experience. No, I was having my baby in the birthing pool at Fraserburgh hospital. It was decided!

It was 4 am on the 15th May, and I awoke as soon as I felt a contraction. I knew what it was, but I thought I'd just lie there and wait because it could have been a false alarm. Glen's alarm went off at 4:30 am; I lay there as he got up and went downstairs. The contractions were still happening about every three to five minutes. I went downstairs, and Glen asked, "What are you doing up so early?" "I woke up at 4 am and I've been having contractions ever since," I replied, and he gave me a great big hug and a kiss and said, "Well I guess I'm not going to work today then!"

It was around 10 am when my contractions got too frequent and strong to stay at home any longer. It was time to head to the maternity unit, and just as I had pictured in my mind, no one else was there, the birthing pool was free, and I would get my water birth! I got into the pool at 11:04 am and Leo was born at 17:10, veiled and perfect in every way. My waters hadn't broken before I got to the hospital, and while I was in the birthing pool, my midwives kept asking me if they had broken yet, but I was in a pool of water and had no way of knowing whether they had or not and, frankly, all my focus and energy was on getting through the contractions. Suddenly, I felt different, and I knew he was ready to come out — and fast. The midwife said, "You're about to give birth to a very special baby; he's still in his sac! Now I need you to push," and push I did. He shot out like a torpedo and then he floated up to the top of the water, still blue and unaware that he was now in a different world. The sac was cut, and as the fluid drained away and his colour changed from blue to pink, his little lungs took their first breath of air on their own. It was magical. I then held him until the cord stopped pulsing 30 minutes later.

It was so surreal. One minute he was still inside my body, the next he was here with us in the world. We had been waiting for this moment for nine months and here it was! Nothing, and I mean nothing, prepares you for the feelings and emotions that flood your entire system during such a moment. Words seem to be so limiting for describing something this wonderful, this special. To someone looking at me from the outside, I must have seemed underwhelmed because I was quiet — I even felt like I went inward — looking at Leo the whole time, amazed by his perfection. I suppose it's like a dream state, and you're not sure what is real and what isn't. One minute you're expecting, the next you're a mother. Not only are you processing that, but your body has been through a major pain barrier, and suddenly there are a million hormones rushing through your system, setting off so many chain reactions for what's to come, and you're left there thinking, "Now we have a life to take care of. Now we have someone that is totally and utterly reliant on us. Now it's time to become selfless." Within three and a half hours of Leo's birth, we were home, and our newest chapter was just beginning.

I loved being a mum from the first moments I held Leo, but no one really prepares you for the rollercoaster of emotions that you go through. No one ever actually says how hard it feels some days, and that you'll second guess yourself more often than you would ever dare to put a number on. And nobody ever tells you about the guilt — don't get me started on the guilt! I'm lucky in a sense because I was thirty-four when I had Leo, so I was mature and sure enough of myself, my abilities, and my inner confidence to be able to understand what was going on in my head, but I know that if I'd walked into the doctors on any of those "off" days, I would have been told that I was suffering from postnatal depression and handed a prescription. Let me be very clear here when I say that I know this does affect a lot of people, and we have to do what we feel is right for us and reach out for help and support. But how many new mums just need to hear what is actually happening? Often, we just need someone to acknowledge the enormity of what has just happened to us. Our whole world has just been turned upside down and inside out because we are now responsible for something that does not come with an instruction manual. As a new mother, you are operating and functioning daily with not nearly enough sleep, no real routine, and often, just as you manage to get used to one that you've put into place, a new stage begins, and so you have to try and adapt to that. We look at everyone else, and we presume that they have it all figured out, that we're the only ones struggling, the only ones feeling the stress and isolation that comes from not really seeing anyone, from feeling like it's groundhog day, and for feeling guilty because you don't have it all together.

The truth of the matter is, almost everyone is just winging it. The truth of the matter is, there is no right or wrong way to do things. What works for your friends and their kids will probably not work for you because our children and we are all unique individuals. The truth is, there is no ideal way except for the way that works for you, and even then, it's trial and error. Like I said, I was able to see this for myself, but it sure would have been nice for someone just to come out and say it because it would save an awful lot of self-doubt during a time that we should be loving every moment, no matter how messy and confusing it may seem.

There is so much that I could write about this subject it would warrant a book of its own, and that's not what this book is about. It's about realisation through awareness, understanding our paths so that we can follow our inner guidance through becoming aligned, and ultimately, waking up to the fact that it's through the inner journey that we find the answers to all of our questions. Having Leo and becoming a mum took me even deeper into understanding my path and what paradigms were at play, what limiting beliefs and conditional patterns had a hold over my thoughts and actions, and the reality that was a result of them.

It was April 2015, and we were moving into a new house. We had manifested this house as our new home from the moment we saw it. Glen and I were meditating every day with the guidance of the same Bob Proctor meditation for about two months. If he was home, we did a joint meditation, and when he was away, we both still did it once, sometimes twice, daily. Even with all the twists and turns that happen while buying and selling houses, we got it. We moved in and with the help of our family and friends we managed to move everything over in one day, which was just as well because two days after that, Glen was going to South America to work for eight to nine weeks. We got all the major items where they needed to be, and the rest was a sea of boxes in the new double garage and an overwhelming amount of unpacking for me to tackle on my own, in a new house, with a toddler. I did it, of course, everything always gets done, but during the process I was aware that my stress levels were on the rise. Yes, it was a stressful time, but I was beginning to act in ways that felt very alien to me, and I was spending the majority of my days shouting at Leo for things and then being wracked with guilt because of my actions, which then had me in floods of tears most nights. I started to have flashes of my mum from when I was growing up;

she spent a lot of her time stressed and angry, and I was starting to see and, more importantly, feel a pattern emerging. This was a pattern that was not part of me. This way of dealing with things was not part of my natural make up and the reason it felt so wrong. That's why the guilt felt intense. I knew I was about to go on a deep journey of inner healing. I didn't know how long this behaviour had been apparent in the previous generations of my mum's family, but I knew it had no place in the future ones.

We have no control over another's free will, and this goes for our children, too. From the moment they are born, they are very much their own person. Our job is simply to guide them and offer information, so that they have the means to make informed decisions for themselves. Even while they're fully reliant on us, their personality is there, and their character and preferences are already forming. And here we are, the adults, thinking that we know everything that's best for them, and when things don't go the way we had envisioned — when they don't follow our instructions or 'disobey' us — most of the time we become reactive instead of responsive, and that is never going to produce favourable results.

I was beginning to understand on a deeper level where my need for control came from and why I would feel a certain level of frustration when I had to deal with outside unexpected circumstances. It was behavioural conditioning I'd picked up from witnessing my mum and her need to have everything exactly how she wanted it to be. There was no room for compromise with her.

Her way was the only way. When she was unable to have things her way, it caused her to become anxious because she wasn't in control and drinking was her way of numbing that, but it only made things worse. And so, the inevitable vicious cycles would grow stronger all the time. Unfortunately, she didn't have the strength of mind required to help herself, so she just kept going.

Had I not become a mother, this is an aspect of myself that I might have never addressed, but it was of huge importance to me. I don't want Leo to have to strip back layers upon layers of trauma and negativity to uncover his true identity. I want him to have as much organic growth as possible in life, and I want his light to shine brightly from within him. I want that for everyone, especially the future generations, and that's why it is so important for our current generations to do the inner work now, to break the negative cycles of our ancestors, so we can move forward into a new age of love light beings. Into a new phase of humanity.

Armed with this new awareness, I was able to start making changes every day to rewire my thinking, which changed my actions and then my results. I made a conscious effort to, when faced with something that wasn't of my choosing (and let's face it, when you're a parent, curveballs come at you all the time), shift my perception to find the positive, new way of dealing with it. Of course, there are still times when Leo's actions test my patience, and there are still times that my "big voice" (as Leo likes to call it) comes out, but such times are now few and far between. And because it hardly ever happens, I am not consumed with guilt all the time, causing even more inner conflict.

Releasing the need to control everything has been one of the biggest lessons I've learned since becoming a parent. It's really helped me to see how I was reactive to situations, and when I was throwing my inner power away instead of being responsive and learning to grow from a situation. It's been another huge piece of my life story puzzle that I've been able to piece together because, not only has it helped me be a better parent but it's given me more patience and understanding of why my mum is the way she is. It's another layer of my onion that has been peeled away, allowing me to get even closer to living each moment of each day in closer alignment to my higher self and my truth. Leo has now become my biggest teacher, and I am grateful for that every single day. He often tells me that I'm the best mum ever, to which I reply, "Only because I have you to help me learn." And that's the truth. He helps me to keep the kid inside me alive. Multiple times a day, I put myself back into my six-year-old shoes to find perspective. Life is just more straightforward when you put your little kid pants back on, and it is extremely refreshing. Strive to be better each day than you were the day before because it's our actions that inspire others, not our words. Be the source of inspiration for others that you want to see in life, and it will reward you with gifts that are more wonderful than you could ever imagine.

CHAPTER 14

~

My Life's Purpose

I always wanted to be a stay at home mum, at least for the first few years until it was time for Leo to start school. I didn't want to go back to work to pay for someone else to bring up my child. Not everyone has the luxury of choice when it comes to this, but I had always held this view, so my situation manifested around this belief, and for that I am and always will be grateful. Children are not children for long, and I want to be fully immersed in every aspect of his growth and development. I want to bear witness to all the new stages, facial expressions, words, first steps, first teeth, everything! I wanted, and still want, my memory bank to be full and overflowing of as much of Leo as I can, and I want that for him too. It gives me so much pleasure and joy in my heart because I know I'm doing all I can to provide him with experiences and memories that will stay with him for his entire life. That is of huge importance to me, as it is for the majority of parents out there. So, when it was time for me to start thinking about work again, I needed to change how things had been.

Before Leo, I had the time and luxury to work when I wanted. Some days I was putting in 12-14 hours, and that was fine because I had nobody dependent on me at home. Now I wanted to earn the same kind of money I had before, but I didn't have the same amount of time in a day, and because Glen works away from home for weeks at a time, the support wouldn't always be there. This was the starting point of me figuring out what I wanted to do and how I wanted to do it. I wanted to keep doing Reiki and crystal healing, and I wanted to get into mindset work because it had done — and continues to do — so much for me. I knew I could help others because of my experiences and the understanding and awareness I had gained as a result. So I made this my starting point and thought about the main tools I was using in my own life to stay aligned, and straight away a thought popped into my mind: meditation. I already knew how to take others through meditation because of my Reiki and crystal healing qualifications, but it was important for me to have an official qualification, so I set about looking for courses. In no time at all, I found a course that was in Scotland, and it was a full day training course which was perfect as I wasn't starting from scratch and already had years of practical experience behind me. The next one that was on was in December, but I knew I couldn't make that one work for me. I desperately wanted to go, but it would have caused more resistance trying to figure out how to make it work, and I could see and feel this; it made more sense to wait for the one in February. I followed my intuition, and of course, it all worked out perfectly. I even had time to start spreading the word while I waited for the course, time to get people interested in classes, and time to organise where I could hold them.

On the 7th February 2016, I gained my teacher's diploma in meditation and being on that course helped me realise that I knew far more about the subject than I had been giving myself credit for, but because I was now armed with a recognised qualification, it gave me more confidence to start classes. Interest was growing, and I knew that I wanted to offer more than just a class. I wanted to give people the power and confidence in their abilities, to use meditation as a daily tool like I did, to create awareness, and raise their consciousness. It was the beginning of my realisation of what I came here to do, to guide others to the knowledge that all of the answers they seek come from inside us, not (as we've been led to believe) from outside sources. Yes, we need to do some investigation work as to what kind of tools suit us as individuals, but meditation is one tool that everyone can benefit from. However, I was also aware that it might be necessary to play about with the different styles to find your perfect fit, so I decided to run a workshop styled event, once a month. I provided information on our energy bodies and how they related to our physical, emotional, and mental states. I taught people about what ailments could arise as a result of being out of alignment, and what we can do to bring them back into a state of wholeness. Each month had a different theme, a different style, and I was able to incorporate crystals into the meditations with grids, crystals for particular chakras, and crystals for manifesting, among other things. I found I had a natural ability to write meditations. I would come up with my concept, meditate on it for ten to fifteen minutes, and then it would flow from me as soon as I put pen to paper. It's a process that I still enjoy immensely, and the results that people see from them speak for themselves.

The monthly meeting was at full capacity straight away, and it wasn't long before I began to run morning and afternoon workshops. People were growing from the results they were getting, things were beginning to change in their day to day realities, they were starting to see the power they held within, and they loved it as much as I did. As time went on, I knew I wanted to focus only on energy work. I wanted to help people become aligned with their higher self, so that they could live a life of purpose, a life that was satisfying, enjoyable, and full of love because that's how life is meant to be. I had let myself become lost in the past, and I knew how wrong that felt, how debilitating it was, and how sad and unhappy I became as a result of being caught in a cycle of attracting all of the wrong things. If I could help one person turn their life around and become their own magic wand through inner awareness, then I would have accomplished something great, and this was becoming my internal passion — empowerment through energy alignment.

One of my friends approached me to start doing meditation classes in her fitness studio. I saw this as a fantastic opportunity to offer the experience of meditation to others within an appropriate space. I kept up with the monthly sessions and even started a fortnightly lunchtime class. All the while, my interest was growing in coaching people, and it wasn't long before I found advertisements for coaching diplomas flashing up whenever I was online, causing me to take more notice. A few weeks passed where the thought would come in, and then it would go, and then more signs started to present themselves, so I signed up for the course and got started right away. You know when something is right for you because you become consumed by it, and I couldn't get enough of my course. I knew I would make a fantastic coach, and that inner knowing was my drive to get through the study. I was already coaching people in the meditation classes, without even thinking about it that way, until one of the ladies in the class said, "I feel like I'm not paying you enough for what I get out of this workshop. You should be coaching people!" To say this was music to my ears was an understatement because I knew that this was a sign of encouragement for me to keep pushing through the moments of doubt and fear that we all face when trying to create something new and step out of our comfort zones.

I worked through my coaching course and gained my qualification with distinction. I then got to work with a business coach to help me set up a website and an on-line presence, and this was when my next stage of stripping back the layers began. I was entering unchartered territory, stepping out of my comfort zone and into the line of fire. I was excited, scared, and full of self-doubt as my inner negative voice began to talk very loudly.

For most of us, when we start something new, the fires of enthusiasm burn very strongly, but at various points, there will be more than one person ready to throw whatever they can on those flames to dampen them, or even to put them out completely, if we allow it. Some people will have the strength of character to stay focused and persistent in the pursuit of their dreams, but when facing such a momentous climb support is needed, not only from others but also from that inner part of your being that knows your true worth — the voice we spend most of the time ignoring.

Not only was I beginning to piece together a new way of working, but I was also starting a new chapter of self-discovery, a new age of awareness. You see, each of us is constantly changing; we only need to look at our bodies for daily evidence of that. But to gain understanding of our growth and our personal evolution, that is something we must choose, and I can see now that I will always choose to understand my journey and the choices I've made along the way at a deeper level because this is my gift. The satisfaction that I feel from joining the dots is like nothing else, and when I see the eyes of my clients light up during those lightbulb moments, the feeling that it creates in my being is one of wholeness and deep gratitude.

It wasn't always this way, and although I had always felt an affinity and connection to the healing work that I did, I was now putting new labels on myself because I was stepping into the world of coaching. I knew I had what it took, but the resistance it created internally was something I was not fully prepared to experience. In hindsight, I could say I made it harder than it had to be; nevertheless, the inner healing I did as I stripped back more layers to understand the limitations that I'd placed on myself would serve me through more hands-on experience, which I could then offer to my clients during their sessions. As long as we are learning from the lessons that life provides us then we are winning, we are growing and evolving. On the other hand, when we choose to ignore the lessons, that is when we die a little more inside each day, because we are creating more distance between our natural state of being and the person we've become. The sickly nagging sensation that we feel in our gut is a gentle reminder of this.

I powered through the emotional doubts that were growing by reminding myself that it was only my ego trying to prevent my growth, trying to keep me small by entrapping me in the comfortable bubble that I had been in. However, that comfort was disrupted by the fact that I couldn't shake the feeling that I was capable of so much more, and I wanted to serve others with the lessons I had gained from my personal experiences. Through my own choices, I was creating so much resistance against what I was trying to do that frustration was beginning to rear its ugly head in the side-lines of my mind. Instead of focusing on creating from my own unique point of attraction, I was comparing my work and my message to others, which serves no purpose other than to squash the very heart of your dreams with negativity and destruction. All the while, I knew I was behaving in exact opposition to how I wished to behave. I had set the wheels in motion, but I was also sending them in the wrong direction.

It wasn't all bad though; in fact, through it all, I was still getting clients, and helping them achieve fantastic results, but it felt hard — the flow was lost — and the underlying tones of hardness that I sensed were causing me to feel increasingly estranged from my higher self. I recognised what was going on; I knew I was creating all of these unwanted feelings and behaviours, and I also knew that if I continued to focus on going in the wrong direction, I would only keep going that way. It sounds crazy, but we all do it. In fact, most people spend their whole lives going round in vicious circles and getting the same unsatisfactory results, wondering why they can't catch a break, or why things that they don't want keep happening, when in actual fact, their inability to change the patterns is the only cause of their dissatisfaction.

As I've said all throughout this book, I knew perfectly well it was me creating this resistance, and I was falling into the trap of trying harder to fix the problem. What I needed was a different perspective to view my situation from. I had been trying to manifest more — more clients, more flow, more creative ideas — and the only thing I was getting more of was being further away from where I wanted to be. So, I turned everything upside down, and instead of asking, "How do I create this?" I asked, "How am I blocking the flow of this?"

For the next three days, I got back to basics with myself. I performed self-Reiki and used crystal grids on and around my body, then I would go straight into meditation, and my only focus was on finding out how I was blocking my flow. It felt good to be back using the tools that had always helped shine the light for me. It also served as a good reminder that since becoming a mum,

155

my self-care routine had been very sporadic. I needed to get back to walking my talk, every day, not just when things were going wrong. After all, everything begins and ends with us. How could I possibly give to others if my own cup was running dry? And how could I get clarity without carving out the time for stillness?

Over the next few days, I had many lightbulb moments, but the major one came to me on the third day. It was a seed that had been planted in my sub-conscious so many years ago that had made a huge impact on me, yet all these years I had been unaware of it. A particular memory came up from my childhood, a comment my dad had made when I told him I wanted to give up playing the bassoon. He said, "Jack of all trades, master of none." It was true that previously I'd learned both the piano and cello before giving up and moving on to the bassoon. I clearly remember at the time thinking, "Why do I have to be master at only one thing? Why can't I sample things to see where my passions lie? Why do I have to pick one thing and master that simply because that's what I started with?" This one comment, and more importantly *my* perception of that comment, had planted a seed in my thoughts, creating a paradigm that made me fearful of starting new things, fearful of adding new strings to my bow. It made me question my staying power. Did I want to change direction because I was giving up on things through boredom or lack of persistence?

This recollection helped me so much in understanding how I'd looked at certain situations in life, how I had judged myself in the past, second-guessed my decisions, and how it affected the confidence I had in my abilities. To be clear, it wasn't my own confidence in my abilities I questioned, but that of other people. I have always known how capable I am and trusted that when I truly want to learn something, I could master it. I had mastered all of the beauty and complementary treatments I learned, even the ones I wasn't crazy about like manicures and electrolysis. I've always been someone who is good at anything I take on, and I take pride in my professionalism. Nevertheless, I was also someone who constantly questioned how good others thought I was, despite all the positive feedback I got.

My transition into coaching wasn't on account of boredom or not having the perseverance to go the distance with the work I had been doing previously; it was my natural evolution. It was me following the signs from my higher self as she guided me to follow the path where I used my gifts to live the life of my dreams, the gifts I was passionate about, the gifts that I feel compelled to share with the world to create more balance and understanding for anyone who desires it. But like everyone else, my paradigms wanted to keep me from growing and expanding, by filling me with self-doubt. It never ceases to amaze me how big an energetic shift can feel from having a simple realisation that comes from a change in perception. And this was highlighting the need for daily study even more because it's through this repetition that we gain an even deeper awareness of and insight into ourselves.

CHAPTER 15

❧

Investing in Me

The next beautifully orchestrated meeting in my life came completely out of the blue, from a post on social media that I had commented on. I can't even remember what the post was about, but my views on whatever the subject was were on the same page as someone who reached out to me. Her name was Suzana, and unbeknown to us at the time, it was the start of a wonderful friendship, written by the hands of fate.

She had taken a leap of faith to follow her lifelong dreams of becoming a life coach. But Suzana didn't want to be just any life coach, she had a vision of working with Bob Proctor and becoming one of his elite-level mindset and success coaches — the best of the best — and through the implementation of the work that she teaches, this is exactly what she has become. It's been such a pleasure to watch her grow. It's so inspiring to see someone walk their talk and to do it with such grace and humility. Despite all her success, Suzana remains a genuine, caring, and true soul. One of a kind she is.

But let me backtrack a bit. I first heard of Bob Proctor while watching the now world-famous movie, *The Secret*, but he's been a leader of modern thought material for a lot longer than that. It's fair to say that he is one of the leading authorities in personal development and human potential out there, and an absolute master in this field because that is exactly what he chose to become. Bob made such dramatic changes in his life simply by learning about and implementing the materials he had learned before sharing them with the world.

The book that changed his life was *Think and Grow Rich*, by Napoleon Hill, a book that he has studied every day for over the last fifty years, a book that can change the minds, thoughts, and habits of anyone willing to put in the work.

Now, I had never been aware of the back story of how that book came to be until I purchased it. I had followed Bob's work on and off over the years, watched his YouTube clips, and as I mentioned earlier in this book, Glen and I used his abundance meditation to help us manifest the house we now live in. And then, one day, I was watching Bob speak about the moment someone handed him the book. His passion for it was so compelling that I went and ordered it straight away. I couldn't wait for the delivery of the book, so I ordered an eBook version of it and started reading it at once.

In a nutshell, Napoleon Hill was challenged to write the book by one of the world's greatest entrepreneurs ever, Andrew Carnegie. As soon as I read his name, I felt the goose bumps start on the back of my neck, then continue all over my scalp and down over my entire body. You may have figured it out already, but Andrew Carnegie was the man behind the glorious Skibo Castle of today. Scottish born, Carnegie returned to his country of birth, and made Skibo Castle the marvel it is today. Skibo was the place that I had a site visit to when I was in my last year of college and the place that I knew I would end up working at, even before I set foot in the place. Believe me when I say that there is magic in the air there. It spoke to me, not just the castle, but the grounds, the trees, the whole energy; everything about the place resonated with me.

When I worked there, I used to wander through the corridors and the rooms absorbing their energy. I loved that place — I still do — and to this day, I have connections there which means I'm lucky enough to get to visit from time to time, and it still feels like home, encompassing my soul like it once did.

For me, reading this book and the history behind it was another sign that I was heading in the right direction. It gave even more meaning to why I felt such a pull to go there. Had I not ended up working there, my life could have turned out so very different. And it was through many synchronicities that happened during my time there, and with the people I met, that I pursued the different energy alignment techniques that I use today, techniques that helped me make sense of my life, turn it around, and find my true purpose of being of service to others in a way that lights up my heart and makes me feel whole.

My new friendship with Suzana continued to grow. We live on opposite sides of the world, she in Australia and I in Scotland, so we started having chats through video calls; she spoke to me about her work and the course she offered. I told her about my energy alignment and some of my history. The familiarity and energetic bond between us was instant. It was like talking to an old friend that I hadn't seen for a while.

Over the next twelve to eighteen months, we grew closer. I gave Suzana some energy alignment sessions, and we spoke to each other about our goals. I'd started to write this book, and she had just completed her own, so her enthusiasm helped to spur me on. I was also tweaking and re-evaluating how I worked with my clients, brainstorming ways in which to make the most out of my unique therapeutic style; I was searching for my energetic career flow, so to speak.

It was then I created my signature treatment, my energy alignment session that comprises of Reiki, crystal healing, crystal keys, and vibrational sound therapy with chakra tuning forks. It was a very freeing moment for me because, although I loved each of the healing modalities on their own, I had a compelling need to create an experience for my clients that was unique and power-ful, and that's exactly what I got from combining my services into a package offer. There are so many wonderful healers out there doing the same type of energy work as me, and it can be easy to get lost in the mindset of competition. My yearning to create a unique way of doing my healing sessions helped me to harness more self-belief and gave me more meaning and connection to how I wanted to be of service to others, for the highest and greatest good, all while remaining true to myself and being a leader in my field and for my clients.

At the heart of my desire to help others was my wish for them to be able to understand their unique energy, to be able to read the signs that the Universe was placing on their paths. I wanted to give so much more than just a healing session. There was clarity forming in my vision for my future career, and the winds of change were blowing again, not for anything dramatic, but for the fine-tuning of the foundations I'd already laid. I was reaching a point where I had done all I could on my own with regards to how I was applying myself. I knew what I needed to do next, but I also knew that if left to my own devices it would be a slower process than I wanted it to be, and I didn't want frustration and resistance to set in. This was a paradigm that sets in with me when creating something new, a paradigm that then creates resistance in my vibration and sees me reaching for the comforts of what I already know.

One day while on a call with Suzana, she called me out on it, in a way that only true friends do. I needed this moment of tough love from her, and I cried because I knew she was right. The tears also came as a reminder that I already knew deep inside what I needed to do. I needed to accept that, sometimes in life, we gain strength from allowing others to help us, when we invest in supporting ourselves in a way that brings out our truest and best colours for all to see. I could have continued to go at the pace I was going; after all, there's nothing wrong with a slow and steady pace — sometimes it's exactly what is required. And then there are other times when you just know deep down that if you don't grab the bull by the horns, your dreams can get buried beneath the layers of shit you've accumulated through life. And then fear keeps us there, scared to break free from the mould we've become accustomed to.

I'd had the time I wanted as a full-time mum with Leo, and I'd made some great progress along the way, ensuring that I was at the right point to take my career to the next level once he started school full time. Now was the time for me to invest in myself again and to take the next step, to turn the page and begin a new chapter. I needed to be accountable to someone, I needed some-one to call me out if I began to procrastinate, so when Suzana asked, "What do you need?" I knew I needed to sign up to her coaching program, and I did.

It wasn't a question of *if* I would work with Suzana profession-ally, it was a matter of *when*. There are so many fantastic coaches out there, with amazing material to offer, but Suzana's course was one created by another former student of Bob Proctor's, Sandra Gallagher, who had also once dreamed of being more than just a student of Bob's and changing people's lives. Thus, the *Thinking Into Results* course was born. It is based on Bob Proctor's study and analysis of Napoleon Hill's book, and knowing how it had changed his life, Sandra's life, and Suzana's, was all the evidence

I needed that the material was powerful and that, when applied correctly, it worked! It also helped that this course would blend in and complement the knowledge I'd already gained and the energy alignment work I was already doing.

It has been the icing on the cake for me to apply myself in the way that I want to, to gain the results I want by working in the way that suits me. It complements what I already do in such a marvellous way, and the more you do it, the more you get out of it in every area of your life. I am so very grateful to the Universe for showing me how to follow my signs through reading the energy and becoming aligned with it, to all the many people who have crossed my path and helped me to learn. I'm grateful for the knowledge that I'll always be learning and growing, that I can never get it all done, and that life's greatest gift is always the experiences we encounter along our journey, not the destinations. Because once we reach one destination, we set our sights on the next, and on goes the circle of life in all its many forms.

The quiet whispers of guidance, the things that you can't fully explain but know are right, the synchronicities that follow us through life, they've always been there, and they will always be there. The choice for us is whether we ignore them and settle for mediocrity and dissatisfaction with the results we see in life, or we follow them with faith that we are meant to succeed, when we allow our hearts to lead the way.

You may have already started your journey to alignment, to feel the wholeness and satisfaction that you know you're meant to feel in life and within yourself, or you may be stuck right now, but you know that there's more out there. My best advice is to let your heart show you the way. Let it light up the path that your higher self is trying to guide you along. Begin by loving yourself unconditionally, and let that love be the first steppingstone. Let it nourish you and light up the flames of passion inside of you, let it overflow from you into your life and the lives of others. Let love overrule the negative forces that prevent you from realising your full potential and being the person you came here to be.

The following is a letter that was written by Albert Einstein to his daughter, and I think this should be made compulsory reading for everyone because the world needs this message now more than ever.

> "*When I proposed the theory of relativity, very few understood me, and what I will reveal now to transmit to mankind will also collide with the misunderstanding and prejudice in the world.*
>
> *I ask you to guard the letters as long as is necessary, years, decades until society is advanced enough to accept what I will explain below.*
>
> *There is an extremely powerful force that, so far science has not found a formal explanation for. It is a force that includes and governs all others and is even behind the*

phenomenon operating the Universe and has not yet been identified by us. This universal force is LOVE.

When scientist looked for a unified theory of the universe, they forgot the most powerful unseen force. LOVE IS LIGHT, which enlightens those who give and receive it. LOVE IS GRAVITY because it makes people feel attracted to others. LOVE IS POWER because it multiplies the best we have and allows humanity not to be extinguished in their blind selfishness. Love unfolds and reveals. For love, we live and die. LOVE IS GOD and GOD IS LOVE.

This force explains everything and gives meaning to life. This is the variable that we have ignored for too long, maybe because we are afraid of love because it is the only energy in the universe that man has not learned to drive at will.

To give visibility to love I made a simple substitution in my most famous equation. If instead of E = mc2, we accept that the energy to heal the world can be obtained through love multiplied by the speed of light squared, we arrive at the conclusion that love is the most powerful force there is, because it has no limits.

After the failure of humanity in the use and control of other forces of the universe that have turned against us, it is URGENT that we nourish ourselves with another kind of energy...

If we want our species to survive, if we are to find meaning in life, if we want to save the world and every sentient being that inhabits it, love is the one and ONLY answer.

Perhaps we are not ready to make a bomb of love, s device powerful enough to entirely destroy the hate, selfishness and greed that devastates the planet.

However, each individual carries within them a small but powerful generator of love whose energy is waiting to be released.

When we learn to give and receive this universal energy, dear Liesel, we will have affirmed that love conquers all, is able to transcend everything and anything because love is the quintessence of life.

I deeply regret not having been able to express what is in my heart, which has quietly beaten for you all my life. Maybe it's too late to apologise but as time is relative, I need to tell you that I love you and thanks to you I have reached the ultimate answer!"

Your Father,
Albert Einstein

I cry every time I read this because of its beauty and its truth. It's the one thing we all want in life, the one thing we all truly need, but we seem to find it easier to follow paths that lead to destruction. What if we did start to love unconditionally? What if we were all taught how to love ourselves first, so that we knew our true value and the value of others? What if we made love the number one priority in life? How much would life as we know it change? But more importantly, what have we got to lose from making love a priority?

We have tried everything else, and let's face it, humanity has been going round in the same circles for too long. We're on the edge of a mass awakening and evolution of our consciousness, and if we're going to succeed and leave a happy world for the future generations, a world they can thrive and evolve in, we had better start adding love into the mix. It all begins and ends with us, first as individuals and then as a collective, but we can only be responsible for our own actions. That's why the love has to come from within first. But I can promise you this, once you accept responsibility and let love be your number one priority in life, the only thing you'll be left wondering is why on earth it took you so long.

RESOURCES

Belly Breaths

At the beginning of any meditation it is really important to allow your mind, body, and spirit the time to get into a state of deep relaxation; this way you are in the right mindset to get the most out of your meditation and prevent distractions from daily thoughts and mental chitter chatter. It also allows you to take in more oxygen, which lowers your blood pressure straight away, creating a deeper sense of stillness and calm throughout your entire being. The best way to do this is through your breathing. Below are the instructions for the "belly breaths" I use on myself and with clients.

1. Close your eyes and begin to inhale through your nose.
2. Let your breath fill up your diaphragm first (you may want to push out your stomach at the same time, until you get used to the feeling of filling up from the bottom first).
3. Then, allow your lungs to fill up with air slowly, from the bottom first.
4. Once your lungs are full of air, hold the breath for a few seconds.

5. Then, exhale slowly and steadily, through the nose.

6. Once you think all the air is out, gently tighten your stomach muscles — this squeezes the last of the air out of your diaphragm, allowing for an even deeper breath the next time.

7. Repeat this process three to five times, each time feeling how your breath gets deeper and longer.

8. Then allow your breathing to return to normal. You will notice that each breath is naturally deeper and longer. Follow this rhythm of your natural breath. If you become distracted during your meditation, let your focus come back to your breath.

Centring & Grounding Exercise

Before you begin any meditation, it is nice to prepare your mind, body, and spirit for the journey you are about to take. I use this as a way to prepare my energy before any meditation, but it may also be used as a meditation by itself. As you practice this, you will be able to do it in a matter of minutes. But to begin with, it's nice to take your time with it so that you become fully aware of the feelings and sensations that occur in you as these change all the time and are different for everyone.

i. Begin by taking three deep belly breaths

ii. Next, visualise a bright ball of golden light. See it in your mind's eye (if you can't see it, then just tell yourself that you can, the point here is that you intend it).

iii. Now, see and feel your ball of golden light at your centre, your hara point, which is two finger widths below your naval. Really see and feel the ball of energy, feel the warm sensation it creates. Become very aware of the energy centre in your body and feel this energy expand outwards from your body, out into your aura.

iv. Shift your attention to your root chakra. See it as a bright red ball of energy resonating at its optimum frequency. Now imagine roots coming out from this chakra, see and feel them spreading down your legs, into your feet and then out from your feet. They push downwards, through the floor, down into the ground; they continue to push through the earth, past all the many layers of earth, rock, minerals, water, all the way down until they reach the centre of the earth. Here they spread out and firmly root themselves into the heart of Mother Earth. Feel how your feet are now firmly rooted on the floor. You are physically connected to the earth. You are strong.

v. Next, take your attention up to your heart chakra, the centre of your chest. See and feel this chakra as an emerald green ball of light, resonating at its optimum frequency. Visualise a flower bud over your heart chakra, any flower bud you like. Whatever comes into your mind first will be right for you. Imagine that the sun is shining onto the bud and it begins to open. This is your heart opening up to the unconditional love of Universal energy. Take a moment to let the flower open up fully and really feel the love pour into your heart chakra. Now you are open to receive and give unconditional love to all life.

vi. Continue up to the top of your head, your crown chakra. See this as a beautiful white golden ball of light. Focus on the purity of this light and feel it open up to the cosmic awareness of Universal energy. Feel your awareness and consciousness expand.

vii.   Finally, surround yourself in the love and light of Universal energy. The brightest possible white light that you can imagine. Know then that you are fully protected and that only positive energy can be part of the journey you are about to take. Any guidance you receive will be of divine nature. The Universe can only respond to love as this is the only energy that it knows. Now you are ready to begin your meditation, enjoy.

Namaste

Chakras

Many people will have heard the word chakra but may not know what chakras are. The word chakra comes from the Sanskrit, meaning wheel or disc. They're energy centres located in and outside of the physical body; each chakra plays an essential role in our wellbeing. Understanding the functions of our chakras and the symptom signs that they show when they are out of alignment can and will help you understand your unique makeup and characteristics at a much deeper level. Below, you will find a beginner's guide to your seven main chakras, located in the physical body, and an image showing their positions and Sanskrit names.

Root Chakra: The first of the seven main chakras, located at the base of the spine in the perineum area, the associated colour is red, and its primary concern is security, basic human survival, and our physical needs. When resonating at its optimum frequency, a person will be well-grounded, healthy, full of positive energy, and have an inner knowing and belief system that all their needs can and will materialise. Out of balance, this chakra can show up in a person as fear, a lack mindset, self-destructive tendencies or bully tendecies, over materialism, or self-centredness.

Sacral Chakra: The second chakra, located between the navel and the genitals, is associated with the colour orange, and the primary function is creativity and emotional balance. When this chakra is functioning in its balanced state, a person will be creative, ex-pressive, comfortable in their sexuality and with their emotions. Out of balance, it can show a person to be manipulative, have an overly high sex drive, consumed with feelings of guilt, hyper- sen-sitivity and have intimacy issues.

Solar Plexus: The third of the seven main chakras is found between the navel and the sternum; its associated colour is yellow, and the main concern of the solar plexus is self-confidence and personal power. It is the first of the chakras that starts to see us move away from the security of groups and begin to develop our relationship with self. When balanced, a person will be confident, self-assured, have respect for self and others and be motivated. Out of balance, it can show up as being judgemental, controlling, dominating, or alternatively, always needing the approval of others, insecure, not comfortable in their own company.

Heart Chakra: The fourth chakra as we journey up the body, found in the centre of the chest with the associated colour of green. This chakra is the seat of unconditional love and compassion; it is the bridge between the lower three chakras (physical connection to ourselves and the earth) and the upper three (spiritual connec-tion and awareness to universal energy and oneness). When the heart chakra is in balance, a person will radiate love; their love is unconditional, and they will have compassion and a magnetic positivity that attracts people to them. When it's not balanced, a person can be possessive and dramatic or even love too much because they fear rejection or feel unworthy of being loved.

Throat Chakra: The fifth chakra can be found at the base of the middle of the neck, and its associated colour is blue. This chakra is concerned with our ability to communicate and express through sound. When balanced, a person will be an excellent communicator and listener and more often than not will have an interest in the arts. When this chakra is not functioning correctly, a person may be over-talkative, come across as either arrogant or very shy, and unable to express themselves effectively.

Third Eye Chakra: The sixth chakra, which is in the centre of the forehead, between the eyebrows, has the associated colour of indigo and is our centre of intuition and wisdom. A balanced third eye will result in a person being very intuitive and intelligent, able to meditate with ease, and aware of their connection to universal energy while having a clear purpose/direction in life. Out of balance, it can cause a person to be untrusting, skeptical, anxious, and fearful of success. Also, anyone who is an overthinker, overly analytical, or matter of fact has a third eye that is out of alignment.

Crown Chakra: The last of the seven major chakras found in our bodies, located at the top of the head (or crown) that resonates to the frequency of the colour violet. When balanced, a person will be very calm and peaceful, aware of their connection and place in the Universe as all energy is connected. This is an attractive personality to be around because of their positive outlook. Out of balance, it can present as lethargy, poor decision making skills, controlling, arrogance, manic depression, and even psychosis.

Reiki

Reiki is a gentle, non-intrusive hands on healing technique which channels the Universal life force energy to promote physical, emotional, mental, and spiritual healing without the use of manipulation. It is a holistic treatment which works on all aspects/levels of a being — mind, body and spirit. It can also be used to help enhance and develop a heightened awareness and conscious connection to spiritual awareness and growth.

Meaning of the Word Reiki

Reiki is a Japanese word (pronounced Ray Kee in the west and Lay Kee in Japanese). The word is divided into two parts and translates as "Universal Life-Force energy, Spiritual energy or God-Directed Life-Force energy.

Traditional Kanji for Rei Ki   Modern Kanji for Rei Ki

Rei means knowledge and wisdom of the Universal life force / God / Creator, which is all knowing.

Ki means life force energy, also known as chi and prana. It is the energy that makes up and flows through and around everything.

Although Ki is omnipresent, Reiki uses the energy at a specific band or frequency of vibrational energy that works with Ki. The specific vibrational frequency will only flow through people who have been attuned to it. The Reiki attunement is passed by a Reiki Master to a student and creates an energetic tube from the crown chakra to the heart chakra, which allows Reiki to flow from Source through the student's crown, third eye, throat, and then heart chakra before coming out through the hands.

History of Reiki

Mikao Usui was born on 15th August 1865 in a village now called Miyamo Cho in Gifu Prefecture. His family was Hatamoto Samurai, which is a high rank within the Samurai system.

During the mid 1800's in Japan, Dr Mikao Usui was the Dean of a small Christian university in Kyoto. He had adopted Christianity as most of his teachers had been American missionaries. During a discussion with his students one day, he was asked if he believed in the healing stories of Jesus in the bible. He was reminded of a statement made by Jesus: "You will do as I have done and even greater things." He replied that he did believe and then was asked by his students to teach them the methods of healing. Because he was bound by his honour as Dean to be able to answer all questions put to him by his students, Dr Usui resigned his position that day, determined to find the answers to this great mystery.

He began his research at the University of Chicago in the theological seminary. After a long period of study failed to provide any answers, he decided to continue his search elsewhere.

As Buddha was also known for performing miraculous healings, he began to investigate several Buddhist monasteries in Japan, which in turn took him to the Zen monastery, where for the first time, he was encouraged to continue his quest there by the Abbot. With no results forthcoming, he moved his studies onto the Chinese Sutras and then the Tibetan Sutras. Studying the Tibetan Lotus Sutras gave him the intellectual answers to the healings of Jesus; now he needed the empowerment. He took the information he had back to the Abbot and asked his advice on how to receive actual empowerment. After meditating, it was decided that he should go on a 21-day fast and meditation retreat to the sacred mountain, Mount Kuri Yama, so 21 stones were gathered for his calendar. After 20 days of fasting and meditating, nothing out of the ordinary had happened, and as he searched around for his last stone in the predawn darkness of his last day, he prayed that the answer would be given to him. Then, out of the sky he saw a flicker of light, and it was moving quickly towards him. Usui became frightened as the light grew larger and drew even closer to him. Realising that this must be a sign, he readied himself for what was to come, and then the light struck him in the centre of his forehead. Millions of rainbow coloured bubbles appeared in front of his eyes and Usui wondered if he had died. The white glowing bubbles then became three-dimensional Sanskrit characters in gold, appearing one by one, and they stayed there long enough for him to register each of the characters. He awakened from his trance-like state filled with gratitude, and in his haste to share his experience with the Abbot, Usui ran down the mountain. He was amazed at his strength and rejuvenation after having completed such a long fast, and as he hurried down the mountain side, he tripped and stubbed his toe. He instinctively reached down to grab it, and as he did, to his astonishment, the bleeding had stopped and the wound completely healed. Once he descended the mountain, he stopped at a roadside stand and ordered a full breakfast, although he had been advised to break his fast with a special broth. He ate his breakfast, and the proprietor was amazed at his lack of indigestion. He then told Usui of the pain his granddaughter was in from having severe tooth ache. He lacked the money to take her to the dentist in Kyoto, so Usui offered to help. The swelling and pain that she had been suffering with vanished, after Usui placed his hands on the afflicted area.

Upon returning to the monastery, Usui found the Abbot to be in great pain with a bout of arthritis. He shared his experience with the Abbot, and as he laid his hands on the areas affected by the arthritis, the pain quickly diminished. The Abbot was truly amazed. Turning to the Abbot again for advice on what to do next, he was again encouraged to meditate. This led him to go and work in the beggars' quarter of Kyoto. He wanted to help old and young alike, so that they could be re-introduced to the society again, receive new names at the temple and go on to lead full lives. After 7 years or so of providing healing, he began to notice familiar faces and asked one young man, "Do I know you?" "Yes," was the response, "I was one of the first people you healed. I got a name, I found a job and married, but I couldn't stand the responsibility. It's easier to be a beggar."

Usui discovered many similar cases, and he wept in despair as he wondered where he had gone wrong. He came to realise that he had neglected to teach the people he had helped about responsibility, and most of all, gratitude. When it comes to healing, the spirit is just as important as the body, and in giving away Reiki treatments, Usui had further impressed the beggar pattern in these people. An exchange of energy was needed, and important, as these people had no feelings of gratitude for the healing they'd been given; something had to be given in return.

The five principles of Reiki were then born from this lesson of enlightenment. At the same time, the purpose of the symbols Usui had experienced in his vision became clear. These symbols were then used to attune people so that they would take responsibility for their own well being, amplify their energy, and increase their own empowerment. He then began to train other young men who would join him on his travels. Around the turn of the century, just before Usui made his transition from this life, he passed on the responsibility of carrying on the Reiki tradition to one of his most devoted students turned teacher, Dr Chujiro Hayashi, a retired Naval officer. The first Reiki Clinic was founded by Hayashi in Tokyo.

In 1935, Hawaya Takata, a young Japanese/American from Hawaii was referred to the Reiki Clinic by her doctor. She had numerous health complaints and a severe lack of energy since the death of her husband the previous year. Whilst in Japan visiting her parents, she was scheduled to have surgery but became very apprehensive about it after hearing the voice of her dead husband urging her not to go through with the operation. It was then she decided to visit the Reiki Clinic where she began to receive treatments and was eventually healed. Takata was obviously impressed with Reiki and wanted to learn it for herself. Up until then, Reiki had only been studied by men, but this did not stop her persistence, and eventually, she was taught the First and second Degree techniques. When she later returned to America, she began her own Reiki practice. Dr Hayashi and his daughter went to visit her in 1938, and shortly after Takata was initiated as a Master Reiki practitioner.

Before World War II broke out, Dr Hayashi began to make preparations for protecting the work that had been done already. Mrs Takata returned to Japan and consulted with Hayashi, and he told her what she would be required to do. Dr Hayashi already knew the outcome of the war and that many people were going to die. Rather than risk being drafted to participate in the war and be part of the violence, Hayashi made the decision to leave his body in full ceremonial dress, surrounded by friends and family. Shortly after the funeral arrangements had been made, Takata returned to Hawaii, where she escaped the incarceration of Japanese/Americans during World War II. None of Hayashi's male students survived the war, leaving Takata as the only person to carry on the knowledge of Reiki. She continued with the teaching of Reiki during a very conservative period of American history known as *the McCarthy era*.

In 1970, Takata began to train other Masters, and at the time of her death in December 1980, 21 Masters had been trained. Takata's granddaughter, Phyllis Furumoto, carried on the Reiki principles and traditions, both as a practitioner and teacher.

Reiki is one path that can fine tune the vibrational frequency of our physical and etheric bodies, which then increases the consciousness of all humanity to higher frequency levels.

Recommended Reading

Reiki for Life by Penelope Quest

The Reiki Bible by Eleanor McKenzie

The Book of Chakra Healing by Liz Simpson

The Crystal Bible (Volumes 1,2 &3) by Judy Hall

The Five Tibetans: Five Dynamic Exercises for Health, Energy, and Personal Power
by Chris Kilham

Wishes Fulfilled by Dr Wayne W. Dyer

Think and Grow Rich by Napolean Hill

You Can Heal Your Life by Louise Hay

Ask and it is Given by Esther and Jerry Hicks

You2 by Price Pritchett

Recommended Services

The following is a list of services I have used personally and can highly recommend. They all offer something different but are of the highest calibre and distinction.

Liam Wood
Rare and Wonderful Crystals and Crystal Courses
esoteric-earth.com

Suzana Mihajlovic
Mindset and Performance Coach
Your2minds.com

Holly Hudspeth
Health Coach and Author
healwithholly.com

Vesna Zuban
Editor and Writer
uptownwords.com

∼
About the author

Laura Morrice is a Reiki Master, energy healer and serial meditator who is on a mission to teach everyone the importance of aligning with and becoming a master of their own energy.

She's been a practitioner of various forms of healing for over 20 years and counts some of the world's biggest names as her clients'.

Laura believes that love is the magic pill for living a life of purpose and abundance, and you can find out more about her work and how she can help you by visiting her website lauramorrice.com.

When she's not helping to raise the collective consciousness, Laura loves to indulge in all of natures wonderful beauty, from growing organic food to exploring the world and its amazing diversity, loving, laughing and learning as she goes.